Understanding
Modelling and
Programming

Andreas Prinz • Birger Møller-Pedersen •
Joachim Fischer • Bernhard Thalheim

Understanding Modelling and Programming

 Springer

Andreas Prinz 🆔
Department of ICT
University of Agder
Grimstad, Norway

Birger Møller-Pedersen 🆔
Department of Informatics
University of Oslo
Oslo, Norway

Joachim Fischer 🆔
Department of Computer Science
Humboldt-Universität zu Berlin
Berlin, Germany

Bernhard Thalheim 🆔
Christian-Albrecht University of Kiel
Kiel, Germany

ISBN 978-3-031-71279-1   ISBN 978-3-031-71280-7   (eBook)
https://doi.org/10.1007/978-3-031-71280-7

This Springer imprint is published by the registered company Springer Nature Switzerland AG
The registered company address is: Gewerbestrasse 11, 6330 Cham, Switzerland

If disposing of this product, please recycle the paper.

To our muses Lisanne, Kirsten, and Karin,
for their continuous inspiration and support.

Foreword

In the vast tapestry of human achievement, few domains have transformed our world as rapidly and profoundly as system engineering. With more and more software involved, system engineering has become a complex, costly and therefore risky endeavour. The underlying technologies for all kinds of interconnected digital ecosystems are dramatically changing our understanding and practice of system development. This is now well captured under the term 'Cyber-Physical System', a combination of the two main drivers of complexity, namely, software ('cyber') and mechanical systems ('physical'). This evolution has not only been about the software itself but also about how we conceptualize, design and model our cyber-physical systems.

Understanding Modelling and Programming is a great book that allows us to better understand the relationship between programming and modelling activities describing abstract properties, desired behaviours, intended structures, needed interactions and other specific viewpoints on the overall system under development. The book is a journey through the intricate art and science of creating the engineering solutions that power our world. Every line of code we write, every architectural decision we make, is a manifestation of a deeper thought process, a reflection of our understanding of the problem at hand, and our vision for the desired solution. Models can very well be used to make this precisely explicit.

This book concentrates on the three core elements, namely, (1) the natural and artificial systems that surround us; (2) models, model descriptions and modelling techniques; and (3) programs and programming. It concentrates on the methodical combination of modelling techniques with programming practice and thus explains how modelling and programming work together and can support each other. It discusses the possibility of combining well-known modelling language constructs with well-tested programming language solutions. Several successful examples demonstrate the combination of modelling and programming in real applications.

The book showcases high-level descriptions that can be used for programs and models. These descriptions have numerous advantages: the resulting 'modelled programs' are much more compact, easier to certify and less costly to develop and can be much easier to understand and reuse and evolve. They may be even understandable for the so-called "citizen developer", namely, domain experts untrained in core software development, to customize or extend their software systems. This book is therefore also a foundation for the currently emerging 'low code' and 'no code' approaches.

One of the perennial truths of system engineering is its dynamism. Technologies, frameworks and methodologies emerge, evolve and sometimes fade away. Using abstract technology-independent 'modelled programs' allows us to sustainably reuse and evolve cyber-physical systems over a long period. "Understanding Modelling and Programming" is an exploration of these enduring principles. It underscores the importance of clear thinking in abstract models, systematic design and the symbiotic, integrated relationship between the models and the programs.

In an age where engineered systems permeate every facet of our lives—from our homes and workplaces to our cities and global infrastructures—the discussed techniques of integrated modelling and programming have never been more critical. This book discusses the foundations and language constructs necessary to navigate this ever-evolving landscape.

May your journey through this book be both enlightening and transformative.

RWTH Aachen
October 2023

Bernhard Rumpe

Preface

We are computer scientists, and we have developed systems using several modelling languages and programming languages. We are also teachers, and we have taught modelling and programming. In our work, we have observed that combining modelling and programming seems to be difficult, even though it is natural to us.

One reason is that modelling and programming communities are different communities: Modellers are not so concerned with programming, and programmers are not so concerned with modelling. Programmers will typically consider code (programs) to be a means to an end, namely, creating a system, while modellers often consider the descriptions to be the models.

Apart from that divide, it appears to us that the understanding of the basic concepts behind modelling and programming is far from clear. Modellers and programmers do not agree about the concepts, even within their communities. In the Unified Modelling Language (UML) community, UML models are translated into programs. This certainly blurs the distinction between programs and models.

Our own understanding is based on a distinction between models and model descriptions. In this view, a UML diagram is not a model, but a model description. On this base, it is easier to distinguish models and programs.

We have therefore designed this book to explain modelling and programming concepts, their relationships, and their use. With these concepts, the modelling and programming communities can come together. Gradually, the scope of our work extended from computer science to engineering, even touching science in general. The concepts in his book are based on computer science, but they are also applicable outside this domain, as shown by our examples.

Purpose

The main aim of this book is to provide a concise overview of modelling and programming by presenting their essential concepts. Our overarching purpose is to foster a better understanding of modelling and programming, ensuring that individuals, regardless of their expertise level, can navigate these domains with confidence and clarity. By presenting a unified perspective, we strive to cultivate a shared language that transcends disciplinary boundaries, fostering a richer and more collaborative environment for both practitioners and learners.

Intended Audience

The book is written for computer science students and teachers. The concepts involved apply to all areas of engineering. Our target readers are therefore primarily engineers using models to create systems. This includes modellers as well as programmers.

In general, everyone who uses descriptions to create systems will profit from reading this book. Descriptions can be code, diagrams, technical documentation or just descriptions in domain-specific notations.

If you work in the areas of programming and modelling, this book helps you clarify the concepts. If you learn or teach about systems, modelling, programming, simulation or semantics, then this book is for you.

Approach

Modelling and programming comprise huge areas of knowledge and cannot be captured in one book alone, even when disregarding their combination. The intention of this book is rather to present the essential concepts of modelling and programming, thus making it possible to combine both of them. For readers interested in the topics we do not cover, we reference books that provide information about these areas.

As a preparation for the book, we have written some scientific articles about several of these essential concepts. These articles helped advance our understanding and were used in the writing process.

We have carefully designed a relevant and comprehensive yet small case that we can use to exemplify all the relevant concepts. We ended up with a case in home automation, which also shows the combination of different engineering domains, in particular hardware and software. For even better practical relevance, a chapter with practical cases is included.

Overview of the Chapters

After an introduction (Chap. 1) to the importance of modelling and programming in the scope of system engineering, the book provides four main chapters covering systems, models, specifications and programs. Each of these chapters comes with a set of reflection exercises. Due to the conceptual level of these chapters, there are no clear-cut correct solutions to these exercises. Still, the companion material of the book provides hints to a solution.

Chapter 2 explores how systems relate to reality. We explore different perspectives related to the purpose of considering the system. In this context, we consider how our systems restrict the interactions we can have with reality, for example, when running experiments. Finally, we consider descriptions of systems and how systems emerge from system descriptions.

In the context of models, Chap. 3 explains what it takes to be a model and how models and systems are related. We conclude this chapter by discussing model semantics, meaning and correctness.

In Chap. 4, we discuss specifications which are precise descriptions of models and systems. We present the language constructs needed to describe systems and show how the constructs can be expressed in concrete and relevant languages. These languages can express programs and model descriptions and combinations thereof. We discuss the concrete aspects of models we want to describe and how we can do this. Here, we consider the structure and the behaviour of models.

For programs, Chap. 5 considers the creation, simulation and execution of specifications (model descriptions or programs). We start by considering the behaviour of descriptions on the level of our system perspective. Then, we discuss ways to create programs for existing and new systems. Finally, we return to the question of correctness, this time for programming.

Even though the example of the book is understandable and can be translated into other disciplines easily, it is still very small and might be mistaken as unrealistic. Chapter 6 presents a collection of real-world cases of modelling and programming. Apart from describing the case, the concepts of the book are applied to the case, giving a better understanding of the concepts.

Companion Page

For this book, companion material is provided in GitHub at the address
https://prinzandreas.github.io/ModellingProgramming.

Acknowledgements

This book would not exist without the continuous support and encouragement of different people in the various phases of the book. To begin with, we are grateful for the discussion with our colleagues in our respective departments. They helped us understand the concepts better and were involved in some of our papers. Our papers led to discussions with other colleagues at conferences and workshops, where we could refine our understanding.

The main example of the book was discussed with many students in our courses. This helped us understand how to explain the case understandably. Justus Mahnke, Arne Wiklund and Abraham Korh helped a lot with programming the room example in SLX, SysML and Python.

When we decided to add a chapter with a variety of cases to apply the concepts of the book, we used the experience and support of Sondre Sanden Tørdal, Dorian Weber, Moritz W. Lemm, Themis Xanthopoulou, Tobias Scholz and Josè Gonzalez to describe these cases.

The book has benefited from the early readers who have challenged our views and contributed in various ways. We are grateful to LeRon Shults, Karin Fischer, Peter Herrmann, Klaus Peters, Themis Dimitra Xanthopoulou, Josè Gonzalez, LeRon Shults, Håvard Haugland Bamle, Terje Gjøsæter, Vimala Nunavath and Arne Wiklund for their feedback on the manuscript.

We also want to thank the editing support team from Springer, in particular Ralf Gerstner, Ramya Prakash and Anju Baskar.

Finally, a big thank you goes to our families who supported us all along and helped solve all the seemingly small everyday problems that occurred over the many years of writing. This book would not exist without you.

Grimstad, Norway   Andreas Prinz
Oslo, Norway   Birger Møller-Pedersen
Berlin, Germany   Joachim Fischer
Cottbus, Germany   Bernhard Thalheim
June 2024

Contents

Acronyms

This section lists the various acronyms used in the book and the page where the abbreviation is introduced.

A	Area	page 46
ABM	Agent-based model	page 84
b	Breadth	page 8
c	Specific heat capacity	page 48
DFSM	Deterministic finite-state machine	page 49
DSL	Domain-specific language	page 65
env	Environment object	page 45
h	Height	page 8
l	Length	page 8
m	Mass	page 48
OMG	Object management group	page 36
Q	Energy	page 47
RTS	Runtime state	page 59
SLX	Simulation language with extensibility	page 65
SysML	Systems modelling language	page 16
T	Temperature	page 16
t	Time	page 42
tT	Target temperature	page 16
U	Heat transfer coefficient	page 47
V	Volume	page 46

Chapter 1
Introduction

> So perhaps the best thing to do is to stop writing introductions and get on with the book.
>
> ―――――――――――――――
>
> A.A. Milne, Winnie-the-Pooh

Our world is complex. Our lives are complex. The systems we build and use are complex. Moreover, they are connected to other systems; they are dynamic, i.e. they change over time, and often their boundaries are not clear. We try to understand and control this complexity [3, 11, 14].

Models are simpler systems that can replace complex systems in certain situations. Therefore, *modelling*, i.e. the creation of models, is a great tool for understanding systems [8]. New systems can be created by *programming*, i.e. creating abstract descriptions of the systems, which can potentially lead to control of complexity [18].

The authors of this book come from a computer science background, where modelling and programming are essential and mutually correlated concepts for *system development* [9]. Modern systems are integrated with existing systems, function in social contexts and include physical parts. Systems combining created (new) parts with existing parts are often called *embedded systems* [16] or *cyber-physical systems* [1].

Created parts can be mechanical constructions and digital applications, while existing parts could be people, trees, houses or other mechanical or digital systems. The distinction between existing and new will change over time—a house might need to be created when there is no house, or it can exist when we want to renovate it.

Modelling is often used to handle existing parts [6], while *programming* helps build new parts [25, 31]. This book intends to clarify the commonalities and differences between programming and modelling in system development by providing an understanding of how and when programming and modelling can be combined [20]. System development involves many more activities than modelling and programming, e.g. project management, but that is outside the scope of this book. A comprehensive overview of these activities can be found in [9].

A. Prinz et al., *Understanding Modelling and Programming*,
https://doi.org/10.1007/978-3-031-71280-7_1

Charlie's Room—Episode 1: *Overview*

Imagine a room placed somewhere under the roof of a house in Norway. It is not a very big room, just large enough for Charlie, a 24-year-old student, who is studying at the nearby university. If you do not have enough imagination, you can also use Fig. 1.1.

Fig. 1.1 Charlie's room (©2024 Joachim Fischer – all rights reserved)

There is a small door to enter the room, which is sometimes almost too small when Charlie comes home from shopping. Most of the time, the door is closed.

Charlie has chosen this room because it provides the luxury of a window. Opening it, the air gets immediately refreshed, which helps during long study periods. The bed is a couch that is placed under the window such that Charlie sometimes can see the stars when getting to sleep. There is a small table with enough seats for the occasional study group meeting.

In Norway, it gets quite cold in winter. Fortunately, there is a radiator in the room to warm it up. Charlie can turn the radiator on or off. When the radiator is on, it keeps the room at a comfortable temperature unless the window is open for some time. At night, the radiator is normally turned off, and then it can get quite cold in the room. In summer, all this is not relevant, as the temperature is just right—not too warm and not too cold.

A common understanding of programming and modelling is important because programmers and modellers often have different views on these concepts, making it difficult for them to cooperate. During the writing process, we understood that the concepts of modelling and programming are used far outside the scope of computer science. They apply to engineering [8, 10, 27, 33] and to many scientific disciplines, like social sciences, natural sciences, economics, history, ecology and education [4, 7, 19, 21, 28, 29].

Therefore, we have extended the scope of the book to cover modelling and programming in general, also independent of computer science, providing a short and comprehensive understanding of the essential concepts in this scope. We cannot and will not strive for completeness but rather focus on understanding and usefulness.

Models are instruments supporting scientists, engineers and, of course, programmers. They are used to describe, prescribe, discuss, design, analyse, implement, enhance, develop, modify, create and maintain systems (see [5, 23, 24, 26, 30]). Many artifacts and thoughts are used as models without being named as such. In the last millennium, models have already led to extensive research literature with many thousand publications. We leave out a lot of possible detail from this extensive modelling body of knowledge, for example, formal methods [13], evaluation [2], use of languages [17] and mental models [15].

We use Charlie's room as a comprehensive case from engineering to explain the main concepts and their relationships. In the context of Charlie's room, we explore several ways of programming and modelling. We will apply the concepts introduced in the book to the case and extend it where needed. The overall idea of the case is similar to the idea of the book: being concise and focusing on the central concepts. In Chap. 6, we provide several other cases from diverse domains to aid the understanding and provide deeper insight.

Apart from modelling and programming, we discuss reality, systems, semantics and correctness. We do not cover these areas comprehensively; you can find more about reality in [32], more about systems in [22], more about semantics in [12] and more about correctness in [2].

We start by discussing systems and system descriptions in Chap. 2. Modelling and models are covered in Chap. 3 before we handle model descriptions and specifications in Chap. 4. Afterwards, we dive deeper into programming including descriptions and their semantics in Chap. 5. Finally, we provide several more examples for illustration in Chap. 6, before providing a summary in Chap. 7.

References

1. Alur, R.: Principles of Cyber-Physical Systems. MIT Press, Cambridge (2015)
2. Baier, C., Katoen, J.: Principles of Model Checking. MIT Press, Cambridge (2008)
3. Bammer, G.: Disciplining Interdisciplinarity: Integration and Implementation Sciences for Researching Complex Real-World Problems. ANU Press (2013)
4. Bellomo, N., Tezduyar, T.E. (eds.): Modeling and Simulation in Science, Engineering and Technology. Book Series. Springer, Berlin (2006–2024). https://www.springer.com/series/4960

5. Boman, M., Bubenko, J.A., Johannesson, P., Wangler, B.: Conceptual Modelling. Prentice Hall, London (1997)
6. Börger, E., Raschke, A.: Modeling Companion for Software Practitioners. Springer, Berlin (2018)
7. Buchanan, M.: The Social Atom: Why the Rich Get Richer, Cheaters Get Caught, and Your Neighbor Usually Looks Like You. Bloomsbury Publishing (2007)
8. Close, C.M.: Modeling and Analysis of Dynamic Systems. Wiley, London (2010)
9. Dennis, A., Wixom, B.H., Roth, R.M.: Systems Analysis and Design. John Wiley & Sons, London (2019)
10. Gianni, D., D'Ambrogio, A., Tolk, A. (eds.): Modeling and Simulation-Based Systems Engineering Handbook. CRC Press, Boca Raton (2014)
11. Gleick, J.: Chaos: Making a New Science. Penguin Books (1987)
12. Gunter, C.A.: Semantics of Programming Languages: Structures and Techniques. MIT Press, Cambridge (1992)
13. Gupta, R., Guernic, P.L., Shukla, S.K., Talpin, J.P. (eds.): Formal Methods and Models for System Design: A System Level Perspective. Kluwer Academic Publishers, USA (2004)
14. Hybertson, D.W.: Model-Oriented Systems Engineering Science: A Unifying Framework for Traditional and Complex Systems. Taylor and Francis (2009)
15. Johnson-Laird, P.: Mental Models: Toward a Cognitive Science of Language, Inference and Consciousness. Cambridge University Press, Cambridge (1983)
16. Kamal, R.: Embedded Systems: Architecture, Programming, and Design. McGraw-Hill Education, New York (2011)
17. Kelly, S., Tolvanen, J.: Domain-Specific Modeling - Enabling Full Code Generation. Wiley, London (2008)
18. Knuth, D.: The Art of Programming I–VI. Addison-Wesley, Reading (1968-2015)
19. Kuhn, T.S.: The Structure of Scientific Revolutions. University of Chicago Press, Chicago (1962)
20. Madsen, O.L., Møller-Pedersen, B.: A unified approach to modeling and programming. In: Proceedings of the 13th International Conference on Model Driven Engineering Languages and Systems: Part I, MODELS'10, pp. 1–15. Springer, Berlin (2010)
21. May, R.M., McLean, A.R.: Theoretical Ecology: Principles and Applications. Oxford University Press, Oxford (2007)
22. Meadows, D.H.: Thinking in Systems: A Primer. Chelsea Green Publishing (2008). https://doi.org/10.5860/CHOICE.46-05-0495
23. Müller, R.: Model history is culture history. From early man to cyberspace (2016). http://www.muellerscience.com/ENGLISH/model.htm. Accessed 30 May 2024
24. Page, S.E.: The Model Thinker – What You Need to Know to Make Data Work for You. Basic Books, New York (2018)
25. Pressman, R.S., Maxim, B.: Software Engineering: A Practitioner's Approach. McGraw-Hill Education, New York (2014)
26. Rumpe, B.: Modeling with UML: Language, Concepts, Methods. Addison-Wesley Professional, Reading (2006)
27. Samuel, A., Weir, J.: Introduction to Engineering Design: Modelling, Synthesis and Problem Solving Strategies. Elsevier, Amsterdam (2000)
28. Schmidt, A.B.: Quantitative Finance for Physicists: An Introduction. Academic Press, London (2010)
29. Sokolowski, J.A., Banks, C.M.: Modeling and Simulation for Analyzing Global Events. Wiley, London (2009)
30. Stachowiak, R.: General Model Theory. Springer, Berlin (1973)
31. van Vliet, J.: Software Engineering: Principles and Practice. Wiley & Sons, London (2008)
32. Watzlawick, P., Birkenbihl, V.F.: How Real Is Real? Confusion, Disinformation, Communication. Random House (1976)
33. Wymore, A.W.: Model-Based Systems Engineering. CRC Press, Boca Raton (1993)

Chapter 2
Systems and Reality

> It's not what you look at that matters,
> it's what you see.
>
> _____
>
> Henry David Thoreau

When looking at the world, we see systems everywhere. We might even say that systems are our way of looking at the world. But what is a system? How do we describe systems? What can we do with systems? How are systems related to reality? In this chapter, we explore the concept of a system as a basis for modelling and programming. We start by considering the relation of systems to reality and how our view of reality shapes the way we understand systems in Sect. 2.1. In this context, we consider the worldview and the purpose of looking at reality. Then we continue with a definition of a system and how systems are used in Sect. 2.2, distinguishing mental, physical and digital systems. Finally, in Sect. 2.3, we discuss how systems can be created using system descriptions. We use descriptions for communication and discuss how descriptions prescribe systems.

2.1 Reality and Perspective

Before delving into the elements of systems, it is important to ask how we can identify a system and understand its relationship to reality. We will explore this by considering how the human brain perceives reality.

Reality is infinite in depth (we do not know the smallest particles yet) and in width (we have not seen the whole universe yet). Given this vast amount of infinity, the brain with its limited capacity is clearly at a loss. The solution is to focus by using a perspective, i.e. only considering essential differences.

Each perspective is a choice of what we observe and how we do it. We can also think of the perspective as a filter onto the real world restricting the things one can see. Niels Bohr expressed it in [22] like this: "It is wrong to think that the task

A. Prinz et al., *Understanding Modelling and Programming*,
https://doi.org/10.1007/978-3-031-71280-7_2

of physics is to find out how nature *is*. Physics concerns what we can *say* about nature." Kant says in [15] that "we ourselves introduce the order and regularity in the appearances, which we entitle nature".

Our definition of perspective follows Kristen Nygaard and Pål Sørgaard [21].

Definition 2.1 (Perspective) A *perspective* is part of a person's cognitive universe that may structure her or his cognitive process when relating to situations within some domain

- By selecting those properties of the situation that are being considered (and, by implication, those that are ignored)
- By providing concepts and other cognitions that are being used in the interpretation of the selected properties

For this book, we want to distinguish two kinds of perspective: the worldview perspective and the purpose perspective as shown in Fig. 2.1. Both kinds of perspectives reduce what we see in reality by ignoring what is considered irrelevant.

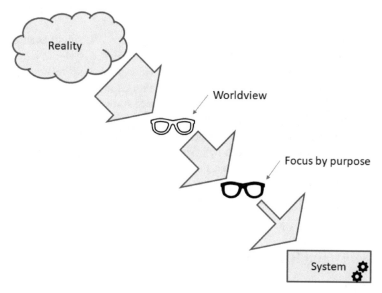

Fig. 2.1 Perspective has the parts worldview and focus, which determine how we see reality (Adapted from [24])

The first part of perspective is the general *worldview*[1] employed. It answers the question: What are the possible states of the world? The worldview is closely related to the language spoken and the cultural agreements in place. It provides possible words and concepts to use together with their relationships [13]. The worldview is a statement about what the world can contain, and it is used to look at the world using

---

[1] The worldview perspective is sometimes called paradigm [18].

this understanding. The worldview includes the physical perception limitations of the human body and the general understanding we have of the world. This again is given by the philosophical approach we use. You can read more about the worldview in [30].

In this book, we apply an *object-oriented worldview*. This means that we identify *phenomena* in our perception of the real world and represent them by *objects* (see Fig. 2.2). Objects may include other objects. *Properties* of phenomena are represented by *attributes* of objects: these may either be data (with states), relations to other objects or behaviours (what the object may do). Classifying the phenomena leads to *concepts* represented by *classes* of objects as discussed in [16] and as given in Definition 2.1.

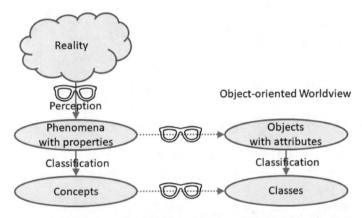

Fig. 2.2 We use a general object-oriented perspective (Adapted from [23])

In addition to the worldview, our *purpose* of observing reality influences what we can perceive (see again Fig. 2.1). It indicates *why* we look at reality. The purpose and our goals determine the importance of the objects we might be able to see using our worldview, and we select only the important objects.

The choice of objects of reality for our purpose is heavily dependent on the worldview, which includes the relationships that might be important for the purpose. Conversely, also, the purpose influences the worldview [30]. This way, a perspective is a structure imposed on reality, given by relevant concepts and their relationships. It is a conceptual understanding applied to reality that influences the way we see the world. Different purposes lead to different perspectives of the same reality [29].

It is not possible to observe reality without a perspective [1]. In a way, we do not live in reality but in a model land, as it is called in [29]. Unfortunately, a perspective limits what we can observe and thus prevents us from seeing solutions even though they are in plain sight. Perspective is a choice, and a well-chosen perspective helps anticipate all the relevant possibilities of reality on a relevant level of granularity. See also Sect. 6.4 for an example of such deliberate and careful choice.

Charlie's Room—Episode 2: *Living Space Perspective*

Let's look at Charlie's room with the purpose of calculating its living space. In Norway, the living space is called BRA (from 'bruksareal' = usable area), and it is defined in the Norwegian standard NS 3940:2012 [26] as follows (see also the left side of Fig. 2.3).

> Building volumes that have a clear height above the floor of 1.9 meters or more and at least 0.6 meters wide are measurable and must be included in BRA. Under sloping ceilings, the area is extended by 0.6 meters beyond the height of 1.9 meters.

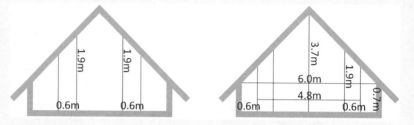

Fig. 2.3 Calculating the living space (BRA) of Charlie's room (not to scale)

The room perspective for the purpose of living space has the following attributes (see the right side of Fig. 2.3). We abbreviate length as l, breadth as b, and height as h.

$$room.h_{top} = 3.7m \quad room.h_{low} = 0.7m$$
$$room.b = 6.0m \quad room.l = 4.0m$$
$$room.w_{BRA} = 4.8m \quad room.BRA = room.l * room.w_{BRA}$$

These attributes are static; they do not change because they come with the room architecture. We only monitor them.

Charlie's Room—Episode 3: *Interior Design Perspective*

We sketch another perspective for the room, this time related to interior design. Now we are interested in the shape of the room (door, window, size), the colours of the items in the room, the decorative elements in the room (pictures, tables, chairs, etc.) and the placement of the elements in the room. This time, the attributes are dynamic and controlled, and operations under this perspective would include moving furniture, adding or removing elements and painting the room.

2.2 Definition of a System

As we have seen, the result of looking at reality with a perspective is a system. But what is a system? The Oxford English Dictionary tells us that a system is "an organized or connected group of things."[2] A more extended definition in the dictionary is "a set of things working together as parts of a mechanism or an interconnecting network; a complex whole". Other dictionaries define the same concept in a similar way. You can find more about systems in [20].

We can also consider an engineering definition, taken from the DELTA language definition [14]:

> A *system* is a part of the world *which we choose to regard as a whole*, separated from the rest of the world during some period of consideration, *a whole that we choose to consider as containing a collection of components*, each characterized by a selected set of data items and patterns, and by actions which may involve itself and other components.[3]

From these definitions and our own understanding of the concept of 'system', we extract the following characteristics of systems:

- *A system has a purpose.* As discussed in Sect. 2.1, the *purpose* shapes our perspective of reality. This means that each perspective, and therefore each system, is a choice of what we observe and how we do it. A different purpose leads to a different system of the same reality. Therefore, a system provides *selectivity*: The system captures only the relevant phenomena and properties of some reality. Because a system is subject to our intentions, we can consider it an instrument as explained in [28]. Read more about system purpose in [6, 9].
- *A system is a whole.* We consider a system to be some *whole*; there is an inner coherence in a system. This provides *separability*: The system has a clear system boundary that allows distinguishing between the inside and outside of the system, where we use the term 'environment' for the outside of the system. A system that can interact with its environment via the system boundary is called an open system. Otherwise, it is a closed system. Our embedded systems are open systems. Read more about system boundaries in [25].
- *A system contains parts.* The whole of the system comes about through its *parts*, which we call *objects*[4] because we use an object-oriented worldview as explained in Sect. 2.1. The parts have a structure when forming the system, which means there is some kind of internal organization in the system. Each of the parts can be identified and can have observable *attributes* associated with them. Often, attribute values (data items) are numbers with some unit and a precision (measurement granularity) and accuracy (acceptable deviation; see Sect. 3.2.1), indicating what we are measuring and how. Read more about system parts and attributes in [27].

---

[2] https://www.oed.com/view/Entry/196665

[3] Emphasis as provided by [14].

[4] Alternative names for the parts could be things, elements, entities, agents or components.

- *A system has behaviour.* In this book, we are interested in *dynamic* systems. This means that the systems have the ability to change over time, which we call *behaviour*. A changing system has different system states at different points in time. State changes can be time continuous (changing all the time) or time discrete (changing only at certain time points). We might call these systems discrete versus continuous systems or combined systems if both kinds of state changes appear. Read more about behaviour in [31].

This leads to the following definition of a system similar to the one given in [11].

Definition 2.2 (System) A *system* is a changing set of active objects that interact with each other and with objects in the environment of the system. Objects may be existing entities like devices, and they may be entities that have to be made. This way, a system is a set of possible executions, i.e. a set of system snapshots that exist at different time points.

This definition does not include the purpose of the system, because the purpose part of the perspective determines which objects to consider for the system, as explained in Sect. 2.1. This way, the perspective determines the structure of snapshots and therefore also executions. We complete Definition 2.2 by defining executions and snapshots (system states).

Definition 2.3 (Snapshot) A *snapshot* of a system is an observation of the system state at a given point in time. Therefore, it is an object configuration of several objects with their relationships to each other and their concrete attribute values.

Please observe how our object-oriented worldview shapes the definition of a snapshot as an object structure with most objects conforming to classes [2]. With snapshots, any system provides a *state concept*: Every situation in the system can be characterized by some snapshot (system state), which again can be split into the states of the system parts, down to the attribute values of the objects.

An execution is a run of a system. The running system can be observed using snapshots of the system execution over time[5] (see Fig. 2.4).

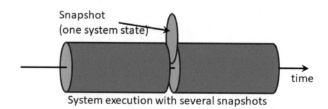

Fig. 2.4 Executions are timed collections of snapshots

---

[5] We discuss time in more detail in Sect. 4.3.1.

Definition 2.4 (Execution) An *execution* of a system is an observation of a system over a period of time with a given time granularity. This way, an execution is a collection of system snapshots at the time points of the time granularity.

Systems come in different shapes and forms. In this book, we want to restrict our attention to the differences between physical, digital and mental systems.

A *physical system* consists of physical objects, for example, rocks, rivers, trees, animals, humans or clouds. It is also possible to have physical objects in the environment of the physical system. An example of a physical system is the solar system.

Digital systems are living inside a computer. They also have a physical reality called hardware, but we choose a perspective that looks at digital objects. There can be digital objects in the environment of such systems but also physical objects. An example of a digital system is a digital booking system.

Mental systems[6] are composed of ideas, concepts and thoughts. Again, there is an underlying physical reality of all the explicit and implicit mental processes. This time, we choose a perspective that allows us to identify thoughts, feelings, habits and similar elements. A thought experiment is an example of an execution in a mental system.

Many systems are combinations of these three types. An architect can see a new mental building surrounded by existing buildings. Embedded systems combine existing hardware with new software (digital objects) running on new hardware (see also the cases in Sects. 6.1 and 6.2). Computer scientists regularly imagine new functionality for their existing digital systems, combining them with mental objects. Even more, digital systems are related to real entities: they represent and handle real objects, like in digital library systems, or they are integrated into the daily operation of real people, like digital project management systems.

2.3 Descriptions and Specifications

We have seen that all systems are based on a perspective of reality. Two people talking about the same situation need to align their perspectives such that they end up with the same or a similar system. We assume both of them share the same worldview.

---

[6] Mental systems are called abstract systems in [18].

Charlie's Room—Episode 4: *Temperature Control System*

In Episodes 2 and 3, we have explored two different perspectives of Charlie's room. The same room can result in a different system by applying a different perspective for a different purpose.

Purpose: Charlie's room can be considered in a smart house context with the purpose of controlling the temperature in the room. When we do this, then the radiator is important, but the pictures on the wall are not.

Environment: In this case, the room is our system. The environment is the rest of the house and the world beyond. From the environment, there is energy coming into the room to do the heating. In the other direction, the window, door and walls will drain the heat from the room to the environment. We see that the perspective also restricts our view of the environment, not only the room.

There are two connections between the environment and Charlie's room: heat exchange and energy use. The heat exchange between the room and the environment does not influence the outside temperature. The energy used for warming the room is provided by hot water entering the radiator.

Parts: We consider the following parts as relevant:

- The system itself is a room object having a temperature attribute.
- A radiator object inside the room object has an is-on attribute and a target-temperature attribute.
- A window object in the room provides an is-open attribute.
- The environment is an object with a temperature attribute.

With these parts, we can observe the following sample snapshot where we denote attributes with their name preceded by their enclosing object.

$$room.temperature = 20\,°C$$
$$room.radiator.isOn = true$$
$$room.radiator.targetTemperature = 21\,°C$$
$$room.window.isOpen = false$$
$$environment.temperature = 5\,°C$$

In our perspective, we choose the unit of all the temperature attributes to be °C with a precision and an accuracy of 1 °C.

Behaviour: The changing of the measured temperatures and the radiator and window states are the state changes in the system. With these objects and their attributes, we can observe system executions (scenarios) as timed collections of snapshots. This can result in diagrams as in Fig. 2.5, showing executions for typical seasonal temperature data. For each scenario, we consider one snapshot per hour for one day. In the snapshot, a blue point indicates the environment temperature (outside), and a green point indicates the room temperature (inside). The window opening is given by a red point, and the radiator on-off is shown with a yellow point. For the last two, 0 means false, and 5 means true. For a better overview, we do not show the target temperature, which is constant at 21 °C.

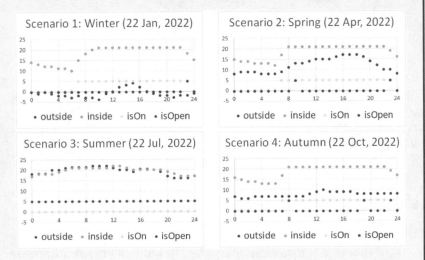

Fig. 2.5 Four sample scenarios of the room temperature control system in 2022, with the outside and inside temperatures, and whether the radiator is on and the window is open

Their discussion will normally include a description of the snapshot or system in question. Let's consider the case of Alice explaining her understanding of some reality (her mental system) to Bob (see Fig. 2.6). For this purpose, Alice creates a *description* of her system. As Alice's system has several possible descriptions, she uses pragmatics to choose one of them. This description is given to Bob, as indicated by the dotted arrows in Fig. 2.6. Bob can now use the description to create a copy of Alice's system, as shown by the solid bent arrow between the description and Bob's system. This is possible when Bob and Alice share the same worldview and use the same language for the description.

What is the process of creating the description? This is done by finding a description that matches best Alice's mental system. In Fig. 2.6, the dotted arrow from Alice's system produces the description, which then again can create Alice's system by the bent arrow back.

Although Alice's and Bob's systems are created from the same description, they can differ if the description is not precise. Therefore, Alice would like the description to be as precise as possible to avoid communication problems.

This indicates that in communication, we use descriptions. In most cases, we assume or enforce that the language used is compatible, such that the meaning of the description is clear.

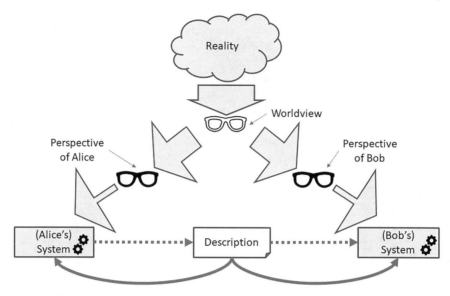

Fig. 2.6 Using a description for communication (Adapted from [24])

As it turns out, descriptions are everywhere. It is difficult to talk about systems without talking about descriptions of them. Even this book is full of descriptions. Some descriptions are informal, as the description in Fig. 2.6.

Other descriptions are more formal, like a formula. For example, we can imagine that the environment temperature follows the formula $f(x) = sin(x)$. This formula is a description written in the language of mathematics. We know that sin refers to the sine function. The formula has a meaning in mathematics, and this meaning is a real-valued function. We can depict this meaning in Fig. 2.7 as a (formal) graph.

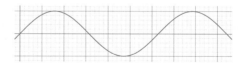

Fig. 2.7 Graph of $f(x) = sin(x)$

The graph itself is also a description, which again points to the same real-valued function as the formula.

This leads us to the following definition of descriptions.

Definition 2.5 (Description) A *description* is a statement or account about the characteristics of an object or system.

Charlie's Room—Episode 5: *Informal System Description*

The description of the room in Episode 1 is an informal description. When we read it, we can imagine a room in our minds. This imagined room is then the mental system created by the description. We can add a graphical description as given in Fig. 2.8 that is similar to the textual description of the system. Note how our perspective shapes the system with its parts and their attributes.

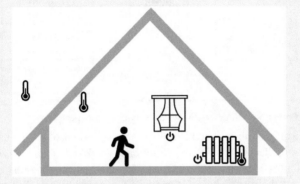

Fig. 2.8 Graphical description of Charlie's room as shown in Fig. 1.1

We could use the description to build an actual room, thereby creating a physical system, for example, a scaled version of the room. As the description is informal, several possible interpretations lead to different shapes of the room systems. A different room for the description is shown in Fig. 2.9.

Fig. 2.9 A different room created from the informal room description. (©2024 Joachim Fischer following Carl Spitzweg, Der arme Poet – all rights reserved)

Charlie's Room—Episode 6: *Formal System Description*

We can also use a more formal description of the structure of the room system using a SysML (systems modelling language) block definition diagram (bdd) as in Fig. 2.10. We abbreviate *temperature* as *T* and *target temperature* as *tT*.

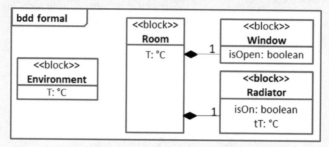

Fig. 2.10 Formal SysML description of the heating system perspective

This description tells us that the room temperature control system has objects of classes (called blocks) *Room*, *Environment*, *Window* and *Radiator* and with attributes T, tT, isOn and isOpen. The window and the radiator objects are parts of the room object. It matches the description in Episode 4 and Fig. 2.8.

Charlie's Room—Episode 7: *Alternative Description*

In Episode 4, we have provided several scenarios of our system. We consider the environment temperature of the spring scenario (22 April, 2022) and collect the values in the following value table, which is a description of the environment temperature on that day.

time	0	1	2	3	4	5	6	7	8	9	10	11	12
T (°C)	8	9	9	9	8	8	8	9	11	13	13	14	15

time	12	13	14	15	16	17	18	19	20	21	22	23	24
T (°C)	15	15	15	16	17	17	17	16	14	12	10	10	8

We can put these values into a coordinate system as shown in Fig. 2.11, left side.

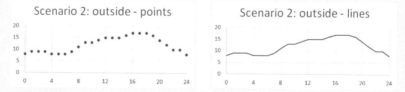

Fig. 2.11 Two diagrams of the environment temperature on 22 April 2022

We can then connect the dots with lines (Fig. 2.11, right). Both diagrams and the value table are descriptions of the outside temperature, i.e. partial system descriptions.

In this book, we distinguish system descriptions and snapshot descriptions. A snapshot description describes one snapshot with all its objects and their attribute values. A system description describes the structure of system snapshots and the possible changes in the system, leading to executions (see Fig. 2.4).

Descriptions can be turned into systems; they prescribe (or imply) systems. In system development, systems are made using various kinds of *system descriptions* from which executing objects are created, thus forming a system (see Fig. 2.12 and [5]). We say that the system is *prescribed* by the description, and we will look into more detail of the 'prescribes' relation in Sect. 5.1.

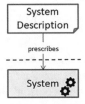

Fig. 2.12 System made from system description (Adapted from [10])

In Fig. 2.6, we have seen that we can prescribe a *mental system* from a description. If the description is computer code, it can be used to prescribe a *digital system*. Furthermore, we can prescribe a *physical system*, for example, a scale model of the room, out of an architectural description. It is important to distinguish between the system description and the prescribed system, as discussed in [19].

The goal of system development is to produce systems by creating system descriptions. Descriptions in system development are often precise and complete. Early descriptions can be less precise and less complete, for example, conceptual descriptions of the system or required functionality of the systems (see [3, 17]). We introduce the term 'specification' for precise descriptions.

Definition 2.6 (Specification) A *specification* is a precise and complete description of a system. It unambiguously prescribes the possible executions of the system in the chosen perspective.

> **Charlie's Room—Episode 8:** *Specification*
>
> We consider an architectural drawing of Charlie's room as a specification of the room. This specification can be used to create such a room or to compare it to Charlie's room. As the description is formal, the interpretation is fixed for people who understand the language of architectural drawings.

Reviewing Fig. 2.6, we realize that the bent arrows from the description to the systems denote 'prescribes' arrows as introduced in Fig. 2.12. Because Alice creates the description to present an existing mental system, we might be tempted to think that the bent arrow should go from Alice's system to the description. However, this is not the case. For the purpose of communication, Alice creates a description, which prescribes a system, which again can match Alice's system (the referent system) (see Fig. 2.13). We will discuss this situation in more detail in Chap. 3.

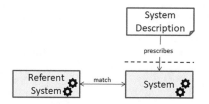

Fig. 2.13 System description for an existing system (Adapted from [10])

It is important to understand that the system prescribed by a description depends on the language used. As an example, consider the word 'gift'. In English, it means 'present', while in German, it means 'poison'. In Nordic languages (Norwegian, Swedish, Icelandic, Danish), it means 'married' and also 'poison'. Another example is the word 'fart', which means 'flatulence' in English, 'speed' in Nordic languages, 'wax' in French and 'lucky' in Polish.

The same is true for specifications. Their meaning depends on the language used. In a computer science context, we consider a box with a name in it. In UML (Unified Modeling Language [4]) class diagrams, such a box represents a `class`. In entity-relationship diagrams [7], a named box represents an `entity type`, which is similar to a `class` in UML. In state transition diagrams [8], a box with a name represents a `state`, while in data flow diagrams [12], it represents a `process`. Such ambiguities are resolved by checking the context and the language used.

Exercises

2.1 (Clock Perspective) Consider a clock somewhere in your household or school. The purpose is to read the time.
Which perspective of the clock helps you determine the time? Which aspects of reality do you consider, and which do you ignore? Which precision of the relevant attributes is meaningful?

2.2 (Alarm Clock System) Consider an alarm clock somewhere in your household with the purpose of reading the time.
What is the system for this clock? What are the parts and attributes of the system? Describe at least one system snapshot using these parts and attributes.

2.3 (Alternative Clock Perspective) Consider a clock on a public building. Choose a purpose which is not reading the time.

Which perspective supports your chosen purpose? What is the system in this new perspective, including parts and attributes? Describe at least one snapshot of this alternative system.

2.4 (Clock Descriptions) Consider a clock on a public building with the purpose of reading the time.
Create three different snapshot descriptions of such a clock. Then describe possible system executions.

References

1. Berger, P., Luckmann, T.: The Social Construction of Reality. Penguin Books, London (1967)
2. Bjørner, D.: Domain Engineering. COE Research Monographs, vol. 4. Japan Advanced Institute of Science and Technology Press, Ishikawa (2009)
3. Boman, M., Bubenko, J.A., Johannesson, P., Wangler, B.: Conceptual Modelling. Prentice Hall, London (1997)
4. Booch, G., Jacobson, I., Rumbaugh, J.: The Unified Modeling Language Reference Manual. Pearson Education (2017)
5. Brambilla, M., Cabot, J., Wimmer, M.: Model-Driven Software Engineering in Practice, 2nd edn. Synthesis Lectures on Software Engineering. Morgan & Claypool Publishers (2017)
6. Burge, J.E., Carroll, J.M., McCall, R., Mistrik, I.: Rationale-Based Software Engineering. Springer, Berlin (2008)
7. Connolly, T.M., Begg, C.E.: Database Systems: A Practical Approach to Design, Implementation, and Management. Pearson (2014)
8. Dennis, A., Wixom, B.H., Roth, R.M.: Systems Analysis and Design. John Wiley & Sons, London (2019)
9. Edmonds, B., Le Page, C., Bithell, M., Chattoe-Brown, E., Grimm, V., Meyer, R., Montañola Sales, C., Ormerod, P., Root, H., Squazzoni, F.: Different modelling purposes. J. Artif. Soc. Soc. Simul. **22**(3), 6 (2019). https://doi.org/10.18564/jasss.3993
10. Fischer, J., Møller-Pedersen, B., Prinz, A.: Modelling of systems for real. In: Proceedings of the 4th International Conference on Model-Driven Engineering and Software Development, pp. 427–434 (2016). https://doi.org/10.5220/0005825704270434
11. Fischer., J., Møller-Pedersen., B., Prinz., A.: Real models are really on m0—or how to make programmers use modeling. In: Proceedings of the 8th International Conference on Model-Driven Engineering and Software Development - MODELSWARD,, pp. 307–318. INSTICC, SciTePress, Valletta, Malta (2020). https://doi.org/10.5220/0008928403070318
12. Hoffer, J.A., George, J.F., Valacich, J.S.: Modern Systems Analysis and Design. Pearson (2020)
13. Hofstadter, D.R.: Surfaces and Essences: Analogy as the Fuel and Fire of Thinking. Basic Books, New York (2013)
14. Holbæk-Hanssen, E., Håndlykken, P., Nygård, K.: System description and the delta language, publication 523. Tech. rep., Norwegian Computing Center (Norsk regnesentral) (1975)
15. Kant, I.: Critique of Pure Reason. The Cambridge Edition of the Works of Immanuel Kant. Cambridge University Press, Cambridge (1998). Translated by Paul Guyer and Allen W. Wood
16. Kristensen, B.B., Madsen, O.L., Møller-Pedersen, B.: The When, Why, and Why Not of the BETA Programming Language. Prentice Hall, Englewood Cliffs (1993)
17. van Lamsweerde, A.: Requirements Engineering: From System Goals to UML Models to Software Specifications. Wiley, London (2009)
18. Lee, E.A.: Plato and the Nerd: The Creative Partnership of Humans and Technology. MIT Press, Cambridge (2017)

19. Madsen, O.L., Møller-Pedersen, B.: This is not a model: on development of a common terminology for modeling and programming. In: Proceedings of the 8th International Symposium, ISoLA 2018: Leveraging Applications of Formal Methods, Verification and Validation - Modeling, Lecture Notes in Computer Science 2018 ;Volume 11244 LNCS, pp. 206–224. Springer, Limassol (2018). https://doi.org/10.1007/978-3-030-03418-4_13

20. Mesarovic, M., Takahara, Y.: General systems theory: Mathematical Foundations. ISSN. Elsevier Science, Amsterdam (1975)

21. Nygaard, K., Sørgaard, P.: The Perspective Concept in Informatics. Computers and Democracy, pp. 371–393 (1987)

22. Petersen, A.: The philosophy of Niels Bohr. Bull. Atom. Sci. **19**(7), 8–14 (1963). https://doi.org/10.1080/00963402.1963.11454520

23. Prinz, A., Engebretsen, M., Gjøsæter, T., Møller-Pedersen, B., Xanthopoulou, T.D.: Models, systems, and descriptions. Front. Comput. Sci. **5** (2023). https://doi.org/10.3389/fcomp.2023.1031807

24. Prinz, A., Xanthopoulou, T.D., Gjøsæter, T., Møller-Pedersen, B.: Where are the models in MDD? Innovations in Systems and Software Engineering, Special Issue on Models/MoDeVVa'22 & SAM'22 (submitted for publication)

25. Rechtin, E., M. Maier: The Art of Systems Architecting. CRC Press, Boca Raton (2011)

26. Standard Norge: Norwegian Standard NS-3940:2023 - Calculation of area and volume of buildings (in Norwegian) (2023). https://online.standard.no/nb/ns-3940-2023. Accessed 30 May 2024

27. Thalheim, B.: Entity-Relationship Modeling – Foundations of Database Technology. Springer, Berlin (2000)

28. Thalheim, B.: Models for communication, understanding, search and analysis. In: Selected Papers of DAMDID/RCDL 2019, pp. 3–18. CEUR-WS.org, Aachen (2019). https://ceurspt.wikidata.dbis.rwth-aachen.de/Vol-2523.html

29. Thompson, E.: Escape from Model Land: How Mathematical Models Can Lead Us Astray and What We Can Do About It. Basic Books (2022)

30. Watzlawick, P., Birkenbihl, V.F.: How Real Is Real? Confusion, Disinformation, Communication. Random House (1976)

31. Wieringa, R.: Design Methods for Reactive Systems: Yourdan, Statemate, and the UML. Morgan Kaufmann, Amsterdam (2003)

Chapter 3
Modelling

> I'm no model lady. A model's just an
> imitation of the real thing.
>
> Mae West

Based on the understanding of systems, we are in a position to discuss modelling
and models. What is the relation between models and systems? What is modelling?
How do descriptions come into this picture? This is discussed in Sect. 3.1. Models
are related to some original, which can be existing or imagined. In the same way,
also the model can be mental, physical or digital. The comparison of models with
their originals brings us in Sect. 3.2 to the issue of model correctness. We discuss
validation, verification, the intention behind the models and their meaning. We
also consider the difference between existing and imagined originals in terms of
correctness.

3.1 Definition of Models and Modelling

We have seen that different perspectives, applied to reality, lead to different systems.
We have also seen that descriptions prescribe systems. Moreover, we have seen that
systems can be similar to one another. We want to capture this kind of similarity
between systems with the concept of 'model' [1, 3, 4, 8, 19]. The general idea is that
a model is an imitation of something else; it imitates an original. We call such an
original a referent system[1].

Definition 3.1 (Referent System) A *referent system* is a system that is picked as a
reference. It is the original we refer to.

A referent system can be a real, existing system, and it can be a planned or desired
system (a mental system), existing in terms of requirements, ideas, etc. Its defining

---

[1] A referent system is called target system in [12].

feature is that we focus on it as a reference; it is the chosen one. Depending on the purpose, even finding the referent system by choosing an appropriate perspective can be difficult, as the case in Sect. 6.4 shows.

We can relate another similar system to the referent system using the concept of 'model'. Figure 3.1 shows that a model is a system (called model system), and

Fig. 3.1 A model (system) is a model of a referent system (Adapted from [5])

it is in the model-of relation with the referent system. The model-of relation is an abstraction relation, taking away irrelevant details. The model system is then called a *model* of the referent system. This leads to the following definition.

Definition 3.2 (Model) A *model* is a system that is in the *model-of* relationship to a referent system, existing or planned, where the model-of relationship means that the model is *analogous* to and *more focused* than the referent system.

Two systems are analogous when they have similar behaviour in their similar perspectives, and a system is more focused than another (analogous) system if it uses fewer objects, fewer attributes or both.

In this definition of a model, the following criteria are implicit:

- Because a model is a system, it always has a *purpose*, and it employs a perspective in order to structure and reduce reality with respect to this purpose. The purpose also differentiates the system from its environment. As discussed before, systems relate to reality via the perspective used.
- A model is a *focused* abstraction with only the relevant attributes. The abstraction is given by the model-of relationship, which indicates which attributes of the model system should be considered for comparison with the referent system. This way, models relate to systems via the model-of relationship.
- A model shows similar (*analogous*) behaviour, which means the model executions cover the referent executions. An execution of the model is often called a simulation (see also the cases in Sects. 6.3 and 6.5).

This way the *model (system)* models the *referent system*, as, e.g. indicated in the language description for the BETA language [13]: 'a program execution is regarded as a physical model simulating the behaviour of either a real or imaginary part of the world'. Often, the overall model-of relationship can be broken down into smaller model-of relationships for the parts of the system, based on the purpose.

We can distinguish physical models, mental models and digital models[2] in the same way as we did for systems. There can be all possible combinations of types of referent systems and models, for instance, a digital system with a mental model or a mental system with a physical model.

---

[2] There are also mathematical models, which are a kind of formal mental models, described with mathematical formulas. Often, they are realized as digital models (see [20]).

Charlie's Room—Episode 9: *Model*

We select Charlie's room system (Fig. 1.1) as the referent system using the temperature control perspective as given in Episode 4. That same perspective can be applied to the alternative room system (Fig. 2.9). The realities behind these two systems are very different, but the matching perspective introduces a similarity between them. The similarity is that they all have a window, a heating device and a temperature sensor.

Therefore, the alternative room is a model of Charlie's room. This extends also to the parts, for example, the window object of the alternative room is a model of the window object of Charlie's room.

A digital model that closely mirrors its referent system in real time is often called a digital twin. In a similar style, mental models mirroring their referent system can be called mental twins.

More often than not, a model is created based on a model description (see Fig. 3.2), which combines the prescribe relationship introduced in Fig. 2.12 with the model-of relationship from Fig. 3.1. The model description is the system description of the

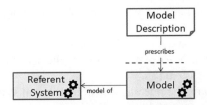

Fig. 3.2 A model of a referent system can be based on a model description (Adapted from [5])

model system, such that it prescribes a model (system) which is then related to the referent system with the model-of relationship. A similar approach is used for system description in the DELTA language [9], where the prescribed system is said to be a model of a referent system. We will discuss the 'prescribes' relationship in Sect. 5.1.

It has become customary to use the term 'model' for the model description, for example, when talking about a SysML model [7] or considering a set of formulas to be a model. It is important to understand that the description itself is *not* the model, but it prescribes the model. Therefore, in this book, we use the terms 'specification' or 'model description' for the description of the model and 'model' for the prescribed model (system).

Having defined the term 'model', we can also define modelling as the act of creating a model based on the goal, the purpose and the usage of the model (see also [16, 20]). This way, modelling is a creative task (see [12]). It is fully possible to create models without creating descriptions, for example, scale models and other physical models, but in our context, models are created by creating model descriptions, so we use the following more specific definition.

Definition 3.3 (Modelling) *Modelling* is the act of creating a model by creating a model description.

In system development, we focus on precise and complete descriptions, which we call specifications[3] (see Definition 2.6). A general model description may be indicative and approximate and may leave room for interpretation. A specification closes these gaps and is normative.

System development will often start with partial descriptions of the outside view of the system, namely, requirements, usage scenarios, relevant objects, attributes and observable functionality. These descriptions are gradually refined with internal realization descriptions until the specification is complete, adding details about data types, event types, behaviour and interactions within the system and with the environment as well as a realization within a platform. We discuss specifications more in the context of programming (see Chap. 5).

There are two main application areas of models, depending on whether the system is existing or planned (see [1, 12, 17]). For an *existing* system, the model is made based on the real referent system with the purpose of understanding this real system. Such models are used in *science* as the core of the scientific method as tools for understanding the real system [2].

For a *planned* system, the referent system is a mental system (the vision of the system). The model description is created and gradually refined until its prescribed model matches the vision. This means the focus is on the model becoming the planned system. Such models are used in *engineering* as tools for design to create systems and realize the vision [10, 21].

Many systems are a combination of the two: they have some existing elements like books in a library and some planned parts like a new book reservation system. A digital library system will contain elements that model real books and elements that model reservation handling. These models will finally become real-world systems being used by real users.

Computer scientists tend to think of systems as software systems, while in reality, very few systems are plain software systems. Almost all systems are either embedded systems including real hardware or related to some real entities, e.g. real books, real people or real money. Therefore, the models have to show a difference between existing and new parts.

---

[3] Specifications are sometimes called prescriptions or prescriptive models.

Charlie's Room—Episode 10: *Model Description Showing Model Boundaries*

Figure 2.8 describes a model of the temperature control system from Episode 4. It takes away a lot of detail that is not relevant to our purpose. We look at a more technical description of Charlie's room system as shown in Fig. 3.3.

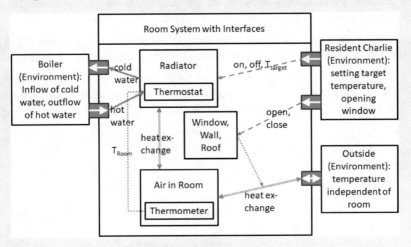

Fig. 3.3 Informal interface description of Charlie's room

The model description illustrates our understanding that the parts of the system only communicate via the designated ports and connectors according to specified interfaces. Looking at the model boundaries extends our perspective, adding the thermostat, the air, the wall, the roof and the boiler that provides heat for the radiator.

The description of the model shows a temperature control room system with a radiator including a thermostat, a thermometer, a window, walls and a roof. The air in the room provides thermal diffusion between the elements. The description shows the causal flow of temperatures and energies, the information and the action flows.

An external boiler provides hot water to the radiator via some pipes and a circulation pump. The radiator thermostat controls the water flow to the radiator based on the room temperature. The target temperature can be adjusted by Charlie. The radiator provides heat to compensate for the heat loss from the room to the outside world. The heat of the air is lost continuously through the walls, the roof and the window. The loss can increase when Charlie opens the window.

3.2 Model Correctness

Models of existing systems can help with decisions in the real world by predicting their effects. This is only possible if the effects in the model match the effects in its referent system, which is commonly called model correctness. However, because the referent system is not the reality itself, care is needed when choosing the perspective. Because correctness is based on the perspective chosen, it is possible that the perspective introduces assumptions that invalidate a match with reality.

Charlie's Room—Episode 11: *Assumptions*

The temperature control perspective of Charlie's room introduces many assumptions that might invalidate our model. We list just a few of them here. Other possible assumptions can be found at https://qr.ae/pyibFB.

- The opening of the door is irrelevant.
- Windy or sunny weather is irrelevant.
- The isolation of the walls is uniform.
- The room temperature is the same everywhere in the room.
- The pipes are ideally insulated.
- The boiler can keep its temperature independent of the returning cold water from the radiator.
- A precision of 1 degree is enough for temperatures.

When the model does not match reality close enough, we can review the assumptions and check whether they are valid.

As a model is made for some purpose, correctness is restricted to that purpose[4] (see [20] and the case in Sect. 6.6). This way, model correctness talks about fitness for purpose, also called usefulness. The model must be adequate for its purpose with the elements it includes and the elements it ignores such that the model results are relevant to its purpose.

Correctness is always a comparison: the model (system) is compared with the referent system, based on the model-of relationship (Definition 3.2). We compare their executions by comparing the related snapshots with the perspective's accuracy. This way, model-being provides structural conformance (see Sect. 4.2) including snapshot completeness, and model correctness provides behavioural conformance (see Sect. 4.3).

Definition 3.4 (Correctness) Model *correctness* is the similarity of the model executions with the referent system executions based on the model-of relationship and the perspective.

---

[4] Models are often used outside their application area given by their purpose. This case is not covered by model correctness, and the predictions can normally not be trusted.

Correctness on the level of models is normally checked using validation as explained in Sect. 3.2.1. If both the referent system and the model are created from specifications, it is also possible to check correctness on the level of descriptions using verification (see Sect. 3.2.2). In addition, there might be emerging behaviours that are not envisioned when creating the model, which we discuss in Sect. 3.2.3. Finally, we discuss the correctness of model descriptions in Sect. 3.2.4.

3.2.1 Validation

Model correctness is about the similarity of all executions of the model against the referent system. We start by considering single executions, which we call experiments or scenarios.

Definition 3.5 (Experiment) An *experiment* is a set of conditions for a system execution, specifying the starting state, end conditions and values for system attributes.

The execution of an experiment in a system leads to a collection of snapshots by Definition 2.4. Experiments can be used for validation and exploration.

Exploration experiments provide statements about the referent system in unknown situations. When the model is trusted, we can use such results to support decisions. *Validation* experiments compare executions (timed collections of snapshots) between the model and the referent system by comparing related snapshots. When the executions match, our trust in the model increases.

A validation experiment has an execution of the referent system and a similar execution of the model, also called a simulation of the referent system (see also the case in Sect. 6.5). The two execution snapshots need not match 100%. The perspective defines acceptable deviations by the accuracy of the attributes. The accuracy has to align with the precision; normally, the accuracy cannot be smaller than the precision. In mathematics, such a matching relation is called an equivalence relation [15] between snapshots. Moreover, the match can only be established for a finite part of the generally infinite execution, maybe by a limited observation time.

Validation means checking a relevant selection of experiment executions. We use the following definition of validation (see also [6]).

Definition 3.6 (Validation) *Validation* of a model is the comparison of some selected model executions with similar executions of the referent system to ensure the model's accuracy.

Validation is the core of the scientific method, where we create models and check their match with observed reality. In system development, validation is called 'testing', and experiments are called '(system) tests'. The referent system here is often a mental system. It is also common to test (validate) individual objects using so-called unit tests.

How many experiments do we need to establish the match? To ensure model correctness (Definition 3.4), we need to run *all* possible experiments. This is often impossible because there are typically infinitely many of them, with some having infinite duration. For an existing system, it might be even difficult to have an overview of all possible executions. Therefore, validation cannot prove model correctness. This means in practice that we need to take into account the experiments conducted when determining whether the results of exploration experiments can be trusted (see also [20]).

Charlie's Room—Episode 12: *Validation*

We select the spring system execution from Episode 4 and compare with the digital model as shown in Fig. 3.4.

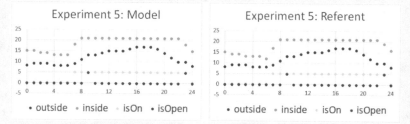

Fig. 3.4 Comparing a referent system execution with a model execution (22 April 2022), with the outside and inside temperatures, and whether the radiator is on and the window is open

We see that only the inside temperature graph is different because the other three attributes are inputs to the model. The green temperature graphs match almost, and the remaining deviations are ignored by the 1 °C accuracy of our perspective.

3.2.2 Verification

In system development, the referent system is a planned system, and the new system being made will be a model of this imagined system. The ideas and plans serve as a mental referent system to validate the new system. We want to create a specification that prescribes a system that is analogous to the plan based on the system perspective.

In system development, we do not only rely on our imagination. The development is done as an iteration of system descriptions, where the next iteration normally refines and improves the previous iteration. A high-level sequence of such iterations is given in [18] as follows. Each step in this sequence can again have several iterations.

1. A requirements specification describes the requirements of the mental referent system.
2. A system design specification describes the system structure and behaviour.
3. A sub-system specification prescribes the behaviour of those sub-systems that do not have parts.
4. A systems integration prescribes the integration of all the system parts.

This way, there is a possibility to compare the partial systems of the various iterations. In this context, the later systems are models of the earlier systems (see Fig. 3.5, which iterates Fig. 3.2 twice). The concrete system is still a model of the

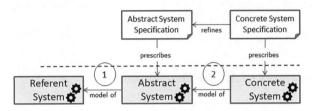

Fig. 3.5 Abstract and concrete models of the same system (Adapted from [14])

referent system but also a model of the abstract system. The same is true for all intermediate iterations apart from the first one. Each next, more concrete system can be checked against earlier, more abstract systems.

All prescribed systems are based on formal or semi-formal specifications. This allows us to compare the systems based on their specifications in a mathematical way, indicated with the 'refines'-arrow between the specifications. This process is called verification.

Definition 3.7 (Verification) *Verification* of a model is the comparison of the whole model with all executions against its referent system. The comparison can be done formally using mathematics if the specifications of the two systems are formal.

Verification is a powerful special case of validation, as it can handle the complete system. It is possible when there are formal specifications of both systems as in part 2 of Fig. 3.5: an abstract and a concrete system specification. In addition, an equivalence relationship between snapshots of the two systems is needed, as verification applies to the common information of both systems (the perspective) (see [11]). For all remaining information, the only choice is validation.

Charlie's Room—Episode 13: *Verification*

When we program Charlie's room system in some programming language, we can verify the program against the specification in Fig. 3.3.

3.2.3 Predictions and Emergence

Exploration experiments in models can be used to predict the behaviour of the referent systems when we cannot observe the referent system itself. This allows us to explore options and what-if scenarios, for example, for future, past or alternative scenarios.

Even though a system is given by its runs, system behaviours might emerge from the runs without being given in the description. This situation is interesting from a scientific perspective because we can describe the low-level rules and we can observe whether the high-level effects appear. As an example, we could explain how traffic jams emerge out of individual driver behaviours or how bullying emerges out of innocent interactions (see also the case in Sect. 6.3).

3.2.4 Correctness of Model Descriptions

For models created from descriptions, we might want to check the correctness of model descriptions. The first level of correctness is well-formedness according to the language. After that, a description is correct when it prescribes a correct model (see Fig. 3.2). We get an indirect relation called 'meaning' between the description and the referent system (see Fig. 3.6).

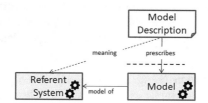

Fig. 3.6 The meaning is a combination of prescribe and model-of (Adapted from [5])

Definition 3.8 (Meaning) The *meaning* of a model element description is the referent element to which the prescribed model refers. It depends on both the prescribed system and the referent system and is hence not unique.

The meaning of a description element can relate to many possible referent systems. So far, a referent system was selected before finding its model, but we can also use an existing system as a model for a referent system. In fact, repurposing models in other contexts is common as observed in [20]. That way, meaning is just a *possible* meaning[5].

---

[5] Sometimes, the word 'interpretation' is used instead of 'possible meaning'.

Charlie's Room—Episode 14: *Electric Radiator*

With our room model, we can observe that it takes the room half an hour to cool down to the outside temperature if the window stays open. We would not want to keep the window open that long in reality. Similarly, we can experiment with different qualities of isolation or exchange the water radiator with an electric radiator (see Fig. 3.7). The behaviour of the room with an electric radiator is quite similar to before, apart from the temperature swinging more than with the water radiator.

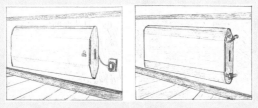

Fig. 3.7 Electrical and water radiator. (©2024 Joachim Fischer – all rights reserved)

The model even tells us that this is due to the water radiator being able to open the valve gradually, while the electrical radiator can only switch on or off. The radiator thermostat opens as follows (λ_w):

$$\lambda_w(\Delta T) = \begin{cases} 0, & \text{if } \Delta T \leq 0 \\ 1, & \text{if } \Delta T \geq \varphi \\ \Delta T/\varphi, & \text{otherwise} \end{cases}$$

with $\Delta T = room.r.tT - room.T$ and $\varphi = 1\,°C$

If the room is warmer than the target, the water radiator is off. It is switched on if the room is more than one degree too cold. In between, the water radiator is switched on gradually. The electrical radiator uses the following formula (λ_e):

$$\lambda_e(\Delta T) = \begin{cases} 0, & \text{if } \Delta T \leq 0 \text{ and } \lambda_e = 1 \\ 1, & \text{if } \Delta T \geq \varphi \text{ and } \lambda_e = 0 \\ \lambda_e, & \text{otherwise} \end{cases}$$

The electrical radiator is switched off if the room is too warm. It stays off until the room is more than one degree too cold. Then it is switched on, staying on until the room is too warm. This behavioural dependency on the previous state is called hysteresis.

Still, the temperature swings of the electrical radiator model are well below the temperature accuracy of $1\,°C$ in our perspective. This means the electrical heating system is a model of the water heating system (and vice versa).

Charlie's Room—Episode 15: *Who Is Charlie?*

Let's suppose our model description only contains a description of an object called *Charlie*, which is of class *Person*, with an attribute *age* = 24. We would readily accept the idea that this description *Charlie* means the Charlie in our room via a prescribed object *Charlie$_O$* (see Fig. 3.8).

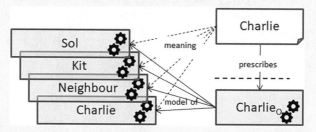

Fig. 3.8 Four possible meanings of Charlie

However, we need to be cautious. First, we must remember that we do not model the real Charlie, but just our perspective of Charlie. Moreover, there can be another Charlie in the neighbourhood, who is also 24 years old. We can use the same description *Charlie* for this other Charlie, making the meaning of *Charlie* this other Charlie, again via *Charlie$_O$*. Even more, if there is a 24-year-old person Kit in the neighbourhood, then *Charlie$_O$* is also a model of Kit.

Not even the meaning of *Person* is fixed, we can consider an elephant Sol, who is 24 years of age as the meaning of *Charlie*. In the same way, the meaning of *age* is not fixed and could refer to the number of friends. These are four out of the many possible meanings of *Charlie*: our Charlie, the neighbour Charlie, Kit and Sol (see Fig. 3.8).

Exercises

3.1 (Paper Plane) Consider a paper plane, folded out of regular A4 paper.
How is the paper plane a model of a Boeing 737? What is the perspective used and what are the behaviours?

3.2 (Music) Consider descriptions of music in the form of sheet music.
Do the symbols describe the music correctly? Which perspective is applied? How does changing the playing instrument change the correctness of the model?

3.3 (Geocentric Worldview) The geocentric worldview posits that Earth is at the centre of the universe and stars, planets and the sun revolve around it.
Is the geocentric worldview a correct model of the movements of the stars and planets? Which perspective is needed to make it a correct model?

3.4 (Heating Model) Recheck Episode 11.

Add more implicit assumptions for that case. Determine which of the given and the added assumptions are valid. How could we extend the model to take care of the invalid assumptions?

References

1. Apostel, L.: Towards the formal study of models in the non-formal sciences. Synthese **12**(2–3), 125–161 (1960). https://doi.org/10.1007/bf00485092
2. Armstrong, J.S., Green, K.C.: The Scientific Method: A Guide to Finding Useful Knowledge. Cambridge University Press, Cambridge (2022)
3. Chamizo, J.A.: A new definition of models and modeling in chemistry's teaching. Sci. Educ. **22**(7), 1613–1632 (2011)
4. Falkenberg, E., Hesse, W., Lindgreen, P., Nilsson, B., Han Oei, J., Rolland, C., Stamper, R., van Assche, F., Verrijn-Stuart, A., Voss, K.: FRISCO: a framework of information system concepts: The FRISCO report (WEB edition). In: International Federation for Information Processing (IFIP) (1998)
5. Fischer, J., Møller-Pedersen, B., Prinz, A.: Modelling of systems for real. In: Proceedings of the 4th International Conference on Model-Driven Engineering and Software Development, pp. 427–434 (2016). https://doi.org/10.5220/0005825704270434
6. Fisher, M.: Software Verification and Validation: An Engineering and Scientific Approach. Springer US (2007). https://books.google.no/books?id=4p0RQPMVuDsC
7. Friedenthal, S., Moore, A., Steiner, R.: A Practical Guide to SysML: The Systems Modeling Language. Morgan Kaufmann, Los Altos (2014)
8. Friedman, L., Friedman, H., Pollack, S.: The role of modeling in scientific disciplines: a taxonomy. Rev. Bus. **29**, 61–67 (2008)
9. Holbæk-Hanssen, E., Håndlykken, P., Nygård, K.: System description and the delta language, publication 523. Tech. rep., Norwegian Computing Center (Norsk regnesentral) (1975)
10. Hybertson, D.W.: Model-Oriented Systems Engineering Science: A Unifying Framework for Traditional and Complex Systems. Taylor and Francis, London (2009)
11. Lano, K.: The B Language and Method: A Guide to Practical Formal Development, 1st edn. Springer, New York (1996)
12. Lee, E.A.: Plato and the Nerd: The Creative Partnership of Humans and Technology. MIT Press, Cambridge (2017)
13. Madsen, O.L., Møller-Pedersen, B., Nygaard, K.: Object-oriented Programming in the BETA Programming Language. ACM Press/Addison-Wesley Publishing, New York (1993)
14. Prinz, A., Møller-Pedersen, B., Fischer, J.: Modelling and testing of real systems. In: Leveraging Applications of Formal Methods, Verification and Validation: Discussion, Dissemination, Applications - 7th International Symposium, ISoLA 2016, Imperial, Corfu, Greece, October 10–14, 2016, Proceedings, Part II, pp. 119–130 (2016). https://doi.org/10.1007/978-3-319-47169-3_9
15. Rosen, K.H.: Discrete Mathematics and Its Applications. McGraw-Hill, New York (2018)
16. Rothenberg, J.: The Nature of Modeling. A Rand Note. The RAND Corporation (1989). https://books.google.no/books?id=wc7qAAAAMAAJ
17. Simon, H.A.: The Sciences of the Artificial, 3rd edn. MIT Press, Cambridge (1996)
18. Sommerville, I.: Software Engineering. Pearson (2015)
19. Taber, K.S.: Science Education: An International Course Companion, chap. Models and Modelling in Science and Science Education, pp. 263–278. Sense Publishers, Rotterdam (2017). https://doi.org/10.1007/978-94-6300-749-8_20
20. Thompson, E.: Escape from Model Land: How Mathematical Models Can Lead Us Astray and What We Can Do About It. Basic Books (2022)
21. Wymore, A.W.: Model-Based Systems Engineering. CRC Press, Boca Raton (1993)

Chapter 4
Specifications

> There's no sense in being precise when
> you don't even know what you're
> talking about.
>
> John von Neumann

This chapter discusses how systems can be described. As models are also systems, they can be described in the same way. We want to describe dynamic digital systems precisely and completely. Therefore, we discuss specifications and static and dynamic aspects of digital systems. First, we discuss languages and specifications in Sect. 4.1. We consider the semantics of specifications and the description of languages. Specification of static aspects is handled in Sect. 4.2 including perspective, system states, snapshots and system structure. Dynamic systems have more than one system state, and their state changes determine the system behaviour. Section 4.3 discusses the modelling of dynamics and behaviour including time, attributes, continuous and discrete behaviour as well as randomness.

4.1 Specification Languages

When writing specifications (precise and complete descriptions), we need to use appropriate languages. We define what we mean by language as follows.

Definition 4.1 (Language) A *language* is a set of descriptions together with their semantics.

It is implied that languages only contain well-formed descriptions. For each description expressed in the language, a system is prescribed. All of these prescribed systems are collected in the semantics as follows.

Definition 4.2 (Semantics) The *semantics* of a system description is the set of systems that the description can prescribe. The language of the description gives the semantics.

© The Author(s), under exclusive license to Springer Nature Switzerland AG 2025
A. Prinz et al., *Understanding Modelling and Programming*,
https://doi.org/10.1007/978-3-031-71280-7_4

When the language used is formal and precise, the semantics is unambiguous, providing unique semantics to all its descriptions. In this case, we call the descriptions 'specifications' (Definition 2.6). Otherwise, the semantics may vary depending on the person or tool creating the prescribed system. In our context, we consider mathematics (formulae and function diagrams) and programming languages to be formal languages.

A language is a collection of its possible descriptions but can itself be described by a language description including aspects like syntax and semantics, expressed in a language description language, which is often called metalanguage. A language description could also be called meta-description as it describes the description.

In this book, the term 'meta'[1] means 'description-of', such that metalanguages describe languages, meta-data describes data and metamodels describe models. This gives us three layers: language descriptions describing descriptions, which again describe systems (see Fig. 4.1). This is discussed further in Sect. 5.1.

Layer	OMG	Room Example	SysML Example
language descriptions	M2	SLX language description	SysML metamodel
system descriptions	M1	room SLX description	SysML model
systems including models	M0	room system	objects of classes/blocks

Fig. 4.1 Three layers of descriptions and systems

Each upper layer contains descriptions (the 'meta') of the next lower layer. The naming of the layers can differ depending on the context. The object management group (OMG) is a consortium dedicated to developing and maintaining standards for software and systems modelling. In an OMG context, the layers are called M0 to M2 from the bottom to the top. The elements in the M0 layer (systems) are 'objects', while the descriptions in the M1 layer are called 'models'. Language descriptions on M2 are called 'metamodels' [12]. This is shown in the SysML example.

In the following sections, we present language constructs that are needed to construct systems and models. They will be sufficient for most modelling tasks, but there is always room to have more dedicated constructs for specific domains, for example, when using a domain-specific language (DSL). We present the constructs in natural language and SysML [10] first and then show them in the code notations of SLX [15] and Python [2] (with the PyDSTool library [7]) as follows:

---

[1] There are many other possible meanings of 'meta', for example, conceptions of something, knowledge about something, classification abstraction, more comprehensive, above and beyond or outside the normal limits.

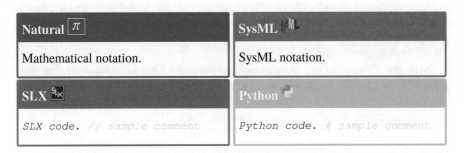

Natural π	SysML
Mathematical notation.	SysML notation.
SLX	Python
SLX code. // sample comment	Python code. # sample comment

Instead of the modelling and simulation language SLX, we could have chosen Modelica [11], MATLAB [13] with Simulink [17] or even the ancient language Simula'67 [8]. We have selected SLX because it is efficient and extensible, Python because it is a popular and widely used programming language and SysML because it is graphical and closely related to UML [24]. The complete executable code in SLX and Python is provided in the companion material as explained in Sect. 5.5.

4.2 Specifying Static Systems

Systems can be observed with snapshots (Definition 2.3), detailing the object configuration of the system state and the attribute values of the objects. Static systems do not change, such that they always have the same system state. Specifying such snapshots is discussed in Sect. 4.2.1.

All states of a system follow some common pattern, which we call the system structure. It is the possibility space for system states: how they are composed of parts (objects), the structure of the objects and the attributes of the objects. Possible system compositions are described in a structure specification (see Sect. 4.2.2). A structure specification is static and defines structural conformance for snapshots (system states).

4.2.1 Snapshot Specification

A snapshot is described by the involved objects, their attribute values and their relationships. In the simplest case, this can be achieved with pairs of names and values. Alternatively, it is possible to use special languages for the purpose, for example, internal block diagrams (ibd) from SysML [10].

A snapshot specification describes one system state, for example, the system start state. Even though a snapshot specification only *describes* a snapshot, it is mathematically equivalent to the snapshot itself, because its structure follows the system structure (see also [1]).

Snapshots and snapshot descriptions have to adhere to the system perspective (Sect. 2.1), which could be described in a structure specification (see Sect. 4.2.2). This means the objects and attributes used in the snapshot description must be given by the system perspective.

SLX and Python do not have specific constructs to *present* snapshots, but they have constructs to *create* snapshots or to *check* snapshots. Below, we show both the constructs to check and to set an attribute value. A snapshot specification needs to cover all elements of the system state (see also Sect. 5.1.2).

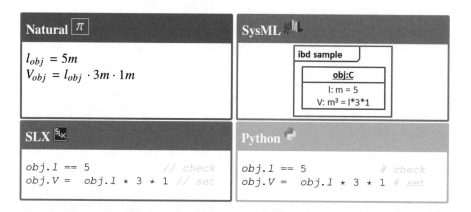

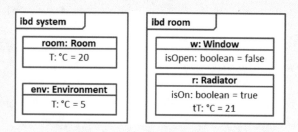

Fig. 4.2 Room system snapshot as SysML internal block diagrams (ibd)

The room has an internal structure and hence its own internal diagram.

4.2.2 System Structure Specification

The specification of the system structure describes the possible parts of the system, their concepts, how they are related to each other and what properties they have [21]. You might remember these characteristics from Sect. 2.1, where we said this was the perspective. This is correct; the structure specification can be considered a formalized description of the perspective used[2]. It explains which classes of objects we can expect in the system, what attributes they have and how they are related.

The completeness and precision of a specification vary depending on the perspective. Specifications on a very high level of abstraction are often called *conceptual models* [4, 9, 23]. With the terminology of this book, they are conceptual model descriptions.

A system structure specification is often based on a so-called "domain model" [16] because most systems belong to an application domain. With the terminology of this book, a domain 'model' is a description of the domain, i.e. descriptions of:

- Phenomena and their classification into concepts
- Properties of phenomena, including their parts and relations to other phenomena
- Relations between concepts including general and special concepts

With an object-oriented perspective, classes represent the domain concepts (and their objects represent the corresponding phenomena), and attributes of classes classify attributes of objects that represent properties of phenomena as discussed in Sect. 2.1. System attribute values can be changed; they are *controlled* (writable). Environment attributes are out of our control; they are *monitored* (read-only). Some attributes are dependent on other attributes; they are *derived* (computed). When we simulate a real system, we also need to control the environment attributes.

We distinguish two kinds of objects leading to two kinds of classes:

- *Active* objects have an activity of their own. They do something without an external trigger.
- *Passive* objects are typically *reactive* – they do not start activities of themselves but react to other activities and follow them up.

We do not handle the individual objects in the system structure specification but rather their classification (templates) in terms of classes (see also Fig. 2.2). Individual objects are described in snapshot specifications (see Sect. 4.2.1). The initial object structure of the system is an example of a snapshot specification.

A system structure specification, sometimes called architecture description [6], has the following elements:

- Definitions of new classes and possibly use of classes of a domain description including identification of active classes
- Definitions of attributes of these classes including their units, precision and accuracy (see Sect. 3.2.1[3]

---

[2] We speak about the purpose part of the perspective assuming an object-oriented worldview.

[3] Even though mathematicians like real numbers with arbitrary precision, attribute values are bound by practical measurement constraints (see also the discussions in [19]).

- Definitions of reference relations and specialization relations between classes
- Definitions of parts of these classes as contained objects

These elements are described in a SysML block definition diagram (bdd), an SLX module and Python classes. Precision and accuracy cannot be expressed in SysML, SLX and Python. SLX and Python cannot express units, while SysML provides a library for quantities, units, dimensions and values (QUDV). SysML marks active classes[4], while all others are passive. SLX marks passive classes. Python does not distinguish between active and passive.

Natural π

There is an active concept E with an attribute T, including an object b of class B, with also an attribute T. A passive concept Y is a sub-concept of H with a Boolean attribute o. The concept B is referenced from Y with the name b. The attributes T are in °C and have a precision and accuracy of 1 °C.

SysML

bdd system

<<active,block>> E		<<block>> H
T: °C		o: boolean

b 1

<<block>> B	b	<<block>> Y
T: °C		

SLX

```
module System {
  class E {
    pointer(B) b;
    double T;
  }
  passive class B {
    double T;
  }
  passive class H {
    boolean o;
  }
  passive class Y subclass(H) {
    pointer(B) b;
  }
}
```

Python

```
class B:
  def __init__(self):
    self.T: float = 0
class E:
  def __init__(self):
    self.b: B = B()
    self.T: float = 0
class H:
  def __init__(self):
    self.o: bool = True
class Y(H):
  def __init__(self):
    super().__init__()
    self.b: B = B()
```

4.3 Specifying Behaviour of Dynamic Systems

The system state of dynamic systems changes due to the system's behaviour. System behaviour prescribes all possible executions, which are timed collections of snapshots

---

[4] The correct SysML syntax for active blocks is more subtle than the one we present here.

(Definition 2.4). We first discuss what time means in a model (Sect. 4.3.1) and how attributes relate to model time (Sect. 4.3.2). After that, we look into continuous (Sect. 4.3.3), discrete (Sect. 4.3.4), random (Sect. 4.3.5) and collaborative behaviour (Sect. 4.3.6).

Charlie's Room—Episode 17: *Structure Specification*

For Charlie's room, we expressed the perspective already as SysML block definition diagram in Fig. 2.10 on page 16. We extend this specification with extra elements to exemplify the elements of a domain specification, leading to Fig. 4.3.

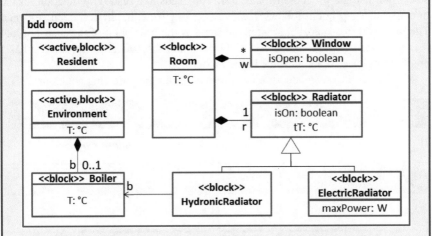

Fig. 4.3 Room model structure as SysML block definition diagram (bdd)

There are three topmost classes, one defining the room, one defining the environment and one defining the resident (Charlie). The room can contain a radiator and several windows. The environment temperature is monitored, the radiator target temperature is controlled and the room temperature is derived, depending on the environment temperature, the radiator temperature and the window opening. There are two options for heating: it can be electric, and it can be hydronic. A hydronic heating is connected to a boiler for the hot water somewhere in the environment. The environment and the resident are active in this scenario.

Please observe that the classes in Fig. 4.3 classify the corresponding objects in Fig. 4.2.

4.3.1 Time in Models

There are two notions of time in systems, which we call *Time* and *Clock* (see also [18]). *Time* is the inherent ordering of snapshots in executions (see Definition 2.4). This way, *Time* is the collection of all possible observation time points, called time granularity in Definition 2.4. There are two different kinds of time points to capture snapshots: discrete time (like taking pictures one by one) and continuous time (like creating a movie[5]). In mathematical terms, discrete time means natural numbers ($Time = \mathbb{N}$), and continuous time means real numbers ($Time = \mathbb{R}$).

   Clock is the domain to read the time in the model (model time). While *Time* orders snapshots and is, therefore, *outside* a snapshot, *Clock* allows to read the time *inside* a snapshot using a pseudo-attribute *time*. This leads to a read-only function for the time in each snapshot as follows: $time : Time \rightarrow Clock$. In physics, t denotes *time*. The *time* read in a snapshot is often the same as the time point of the snapshot, but it can deviate when the model uses slow motion or fast forward. Moreover, it has a precision as every other attribute in the model.

   The *time* function (model time) can be read using the following notations:

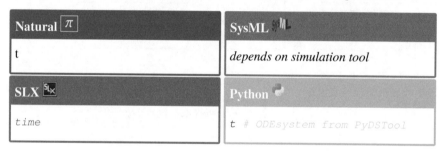

Natural π	SysML
t	*depends on simulation tool*
SLX	**Python**
`time`	`t  # ODEsystem from PyDSTool`

For completeness, we consider another *Time* domain called real-time. This is the *Time* we know in reality and measure with a regular clock, i.e. the *Time* outside the model. The *Time* in the model often deviates from real time for several reasons:

- If the modelled reality is very quick (e.g. quick movements or effects on the level of atoms), then the model will not be fast enough to do the proper calculations. This way, the real time will be too fast for the model.
- Conversely, if we model very long-term reality (e.g. climate models), then the real time is much too slow, and we would have to wait too long for time to pass. For weather models, it is the key point that we can advance the model *time*.
- Sometimes, an activity in the model must start at an exact time point. This is difficult to achieve when the real-time is running independently.

---

[5] Actual movies are sequences of discrete pictures. We refer here to the idea of a continuous stream of snapshots without breaks.

Typically, *time*, also called *model time*, is read from a centralized clock that all parts of the system can access. Alternatively, in distributed systems [26], we can also use relative *time* with several clocks as introduced by Einstein. A comprehensive treatment of time and its axioms is provided in [3].

The main kinds of *time* in systems are as follows:

no time: $Time = \mathbb{N}, Clock = \emptyset$ The easiest situation is when *time* is not read in snapshots because it is irrelevant. This can be the case for causal systems without time-related dependencies.

discrete time: $Time = \mathbb{N}, Clock = \mathbb{Q}$ Discrete time is granular, and time progresses with the number of snapshots. In discrete time, the *time* function can move at the same rate as the snapshots (with a *time* sequence like $(0, 1, 2, 3, 4, ...)$), faster than the snapshots (fast forward with a *time* sequence like $(0, 1, 3, 6, 7, ...)$) or slower than the snapshots (slow motion with a *time* sequence like $(0, 1, 1, 1, 2, 3, 3, 4, ...)$). The clock can also show negative numbers or fractions.

continuous time: $TIME = \mathbb{R}, CLOCK = \mathbb{R}$ In continuous time, the *time* function yields a real number that matches the time point of the snapshot, such that $time(t) = t$.

real time: $Time = \mathbb{N}, Clock = \mathbb{Q}$ Lastly, it is possible to use real-time as it is accessible on any clock, for example, on the computer: $time(t) = realtime()$. Using real time can lead to different time readings in the same snapshot.

Please note that we avoid the philosophical question of whether physical time is continuous or discrete as discussed in [19]. We only need to know that we can access *time* using a clock. If you are interested in the physics of time, please check [20].

Charlie's Room—Episode 18: *Time*

The radiator in Charlie's room is independent of time (no time) – it only depends on the room temperature, which means we can use a no time approach. Charlie has a schedule based on a discrete clock, which means discrete time would work here. The room temperature changes continuously, such that continuous time is needed. Therefore, our room system uses a centralized clock called *t* with continuous time.

4.3.2 Behaviour of Attributes

Each attribute identified in the system structure specification provides a value in each snapshot (system state), i.e. for each time point (see Definition 2.4). Therefore, in a mathematical understanding, each attribute is a function over all possible model time points. On this basis, we consider each attribute *att* of unit U as a function from the *Time* domain to the domain of the attribute itself: $att : Time \rightarrow U$. In this book, we use the names of the attributes as names for their related functions. Using mathematical formulas, we can define the values of controlled attribute functions.

First, we look at simple constant functions that do not use time. They are specified as simple mathematical expressions like $f(t) = 20$. Because they are independent of time, we can write $f = 20$. Other functions can be calculated by only taking into account the current model time. They can be specified by their time expression, for example, $f(t) = \texttt{sin}(t)$. Such specifications are already shown in Sect. 4.2.1.

An attribute function can also be defined by a value table as follows:

	6	7	8	9	10	11	12
f	-4	-4	-3	-1	2	10	23
g	2	16	4	20	8	23	0
h	21	19	17	14	17	19	21

A value table relates to discrete time. If we use continuous time, we can extend the value table to a complete function by keeping the previous value until the new value is available (constant interpolation), by connecting two adjacent values with a straight line (linear interpolation) or by connecting them with a smooth line (spline interpolation). Figure 4.4 shows these alternatives.

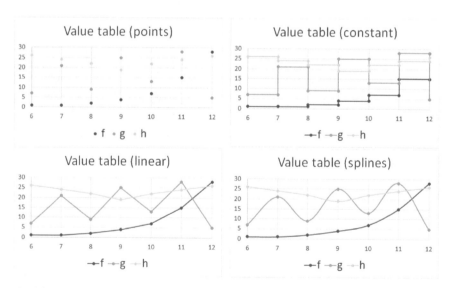

Fig. 4.4 Diagrams of the data from the value table with different interpolations

Value tables can be programmed as attribute changes (see Sect. 4.2.1). It is possible to use libraries to simplify the handling as in SLX below.

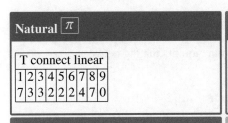

Natural $\boxed{\pi}$

T connect linear								
1	2	3	4	5	6	7	8	9
7	3	3	2	2	2	4	7	0

SysML

In SysML, value tables have to be programmed as attribute changes using discrete or continuous behaviour.

SLX

```
ValueTable T_values(Hour);

fill T_values with
   (1,7), (2,3), (3,3),
   (4,2), (5,2), (6,2),
   (7,4), (8,7), (9,0);

T.state =
   T_values.linear(time);
```

Python

```
T_values: ValueTable =
      ValueTable(Hour)
T_values.fill_values(
      (1,7), (2,3), (3,3),
      (4,2), (5,2), (6,2),
      (7,4), (8,7), (9,0)
)
# could read from csv file
T.state = T_values.linear(t);
```

Charlie's Room—Episode 19: *Simple Attribute Functions*

From Episode 18, we know that we use continuous time. Therefore, attribute functions are time-continuous. The system structure specification in Fig. 4.3 introduces the following functions, when we assume an object *room* of class *Room* and an object *env* of class *Environment*:

$$room.T : TIME \rightarrow \mathbb{R}$$
$$room.r.isOn : TIME \rightarrow \mathbb{B}$$
$$room.r.tT : TIME \rightarrow \mathbb{R}$$
$$room.w.isOpen : TIME \rightarrow \mathbb{B}$$
$$env.T : TIME \rightarrow \mathbb{R}$$
$$env.b.T : TIME \rightarrow \mathbb{R}$$

The domains used for the functions are real numbers ($\mathbb{R}$) and logical (Boolean) values ($\mathbb{B}$). It would also be possible to use natural numbers ($\mathbb{N}$), integers ($\mathbb{Z}$) or enumeration domains.

The values of the function *room.T* are discussed in Sect. 4.3.3, function *room.r.isOn* in Sect. 4.3.4, function *room.r.tT* in Chap. 5 and function *room.w.isOpen* in Sects. 4.3.4 and 4.3.5.

The boiler temperature (in °C) is monitored and needs to be set in the model environment. For simplicity, we use a constant temperature as follows:

$$env.b.T(t) = 40$$

The environment temperature (in °C) is also monitored. For a simple experiment, we could use an adapted sine function fluctuating between 5 at 4:00 a.m. and 15 at 4:00 p.m. as follows:

$$env.T(t) = 5sin(2\pi(t - 10)/24) + 10$$

In this formula, *sin* refers to the sine function, while π is a number constant with a value of 3.1415....

Alternatively, we can use the past temperature values from Episode 4 in a value table. We could similarly use a temperature forecast.

Date	1	2	3	4	5	6	7	8	9	10	11	12
Jan 22, 2022	-1	0	-1	-2	-2	-3	-2	-3	-3	-4	-1	0
Apr 22, 2022	9	9	9	8	8	8	9	11	13	13	14	15
Jul 22, 2022	18	18	20	20	21	21	21	21	22	22	22	21
Oct 22, 2022	6	6	7	7	7	7	7	7	7	7	8	9

Date	13	14	15	16	17	18	19	20	21	22	23	24
Jan 22, 2022	2	3	4	2	0	-1	-2	-2	-3	-2	-2	-1
Apr 22, 2022	15	15	16	17	17	17	16	14	12	10	10	8
Jul 22, 2022	20	20	19	20	20	20	19	17	16	16	16	17
Oct 22, 2022.	10	9	9	9	9	8	8	8	8	8	8	8

For the next episodes, we need the following geometric constants about volumes (V) and areas (A), where we indicate the units used. Some values are derived from the values available in Episode 2, while others are directly given as controlled values. A_{wa} and A_{ro} are the areas of wall and roof, respectively.

$$room.V : m^3 = room.l \cdot room.b \cdot \frac{room.h_{top} + room.h_{low}}{2}$$

$$room.A_{wa} : m^2 = 18.8$$

$$room.A_{ro} : m^2 = 2 \cdot room.l \cdot \sqrt{2} \cdot (room.h_{top} - room.h_{low})$$

$$room.r.A : m^2 = 4$$

$$room.r.V : l = 10$$

$$room.w.A : m^2 = 1.4$$

4.3.3 Continuous Behaviour

For complex systems, it is often difficult or even impossible to compute the value of an attribute directly. In many cases, however, the function's *rate of change* is known, thus defining the function indirectly. This principle is often applied in physics using interrelated ordinary first-order differential equations to express such functions. Instead of directly defining $f(t)$, we define its change rate called $f'(t)$, which implicitly defines $f(t)$. This is only possible with a continuous time domain. In addition to the change rate, which states how the next value depends on the previous values, an initial value of the function is needed to start the computation.

We show the notation for an example of three functions f, g and h, where f and g are defined using their derivatives f' and g', while h is a directly controlled attribute function. The definition of initial values was explained in Sect. 4.2.1.

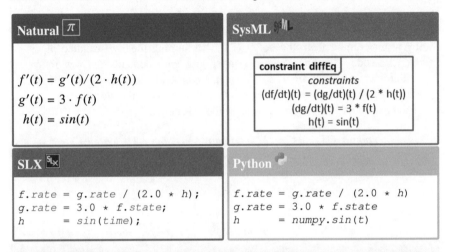

Natural π

$f'(t) = g'(t)/(2 \cdot h(t))$
$g'(t) = 3 \cdot f(t)$
$h(t) = sin(t)$

SysML

constraint diffEq
constraints
(df/dt)(t) = (dg/dt)(t) / (2 * h(t))
(dg/dt)(t) = 3 * f(t)
h(t) = sin(t)

SLX

```
f.rate = g.rate / (2.0 * h);
g.rate = 3.0 * f.state;
h      = sin(time);
```

Python

```
f.rate = g.rate / (2.0 * h)
g.rate = 3.0 * f.state
h      = numpy.sin(t)
```

Charlie's Room—Episode 20: *Temperature Dependencies*

We use mutually dependent differential equations for the radiator and room temperatures based on the outside temperature. The air in the room provides thermal diffusion between its elements, levelling their energy.

Newton's law of cooling [22] states that the rate of heat energy change of a body is proportional to the temperature difference between the body and its surroundings as follows: $Q' = U \cdot A \cdot (T - env.T)$. As usual, Q is the energy, A is the area and U is the heat transfer coefficient, assumed to be independent of the temperature. This gives the room energy change by subtracting the energy losses of the window (Q'_{wi}), the wall (Q'_{wa}) and the roof (Q'_{ro}) from the energy gain of the radiator ($room.r.Q'$). All energy changes are given as Joule per second (J/s).

$$room.Q' : \text{J/s} = room.r.Q' - Q'_{wi} - Q'_{wa} - Q'_{ro}$$
$$Q'_{wi} : \text{J/s} = U_{wi} \cdot room.w.A \cdot (room.T - env.T)$$
$$Q'_{wa} : \text{J/s} = U_{wa} \cdot room.A_{wa} \cdot (room.T - env.T)$$
$$Q'_{ro} : \text{J/s} = U_{ro} \cdot room.A_{ro} \cdot (room.T - env.T)$$

From the energy change, we can calculate the temperature change by the thermal energy equation: $Q' = m \cdot c \cdot T'$, where m is the mass and c is the specific heat capacity. The mass of a physical object can be calculated by multiplying its volume (V) with its density (called δ): $m = V \cdot \delta$. This gives us the room temperature change.

$$room.T' : {}^\circ C/s = \frac{room.Q'}{room.V \cdot \delta_{air} \cdot c_{air}}$$

The radiator loses temperature to the room (T_{loss}) and gains temperature by water coming from the boiler (T_{gain}) assuming ideally insulated pipes (see Episode 11). The radiator temperature gain depends on how much radiator water is replaced by boiler water, which again depends on the radiator thermostat opening λ (see Episode 14) and the maximal water flow f_{water}. The heat transfer coefficient for the radiator is called U_{ra}.

$$room.r.Q' : \ J/s \ = U_{ra} \cdot room.r.A \cdot (room.r.T - room.T)$$

$$room.r.T' : {}^\circ C/s = T'_{gain} - T'_{loss}$$

$$T'_{gain} : {}^\circ C/s = \frac{\lambda \cdot f_{water}}{room.r.V} \cdot (env.b.T - room.r.T)$$

$$T'_{loss} : {}^\circ C/s = \frac{room.r.Q'}{room.r.V \cdot \delta_{water} \cdot c_{water}}$$

Some constants are universal. We find the remaining constants in the radiator, circulation pump, window and house documentation. There are two heat transfer coefficients for the window, open and closed, where the open case is heat exchange in open air.

$$
\begin{aligned}
\delta_{water} &: \quad kg/l \quad = 1 \\
\delta_{air} &: \quad kg/m^3 \quad = 1.204 \\
c_{water} &: \quad J/kg/{}^\circ C \quad = 4184 \\
c_{air} &: \quad J/kg/{}^\circ C \quad = 1004 \\
f_{water} &: \quad l/s \quad = 0.5 \\
U_{ra} &: J/m^2/{}^\circ C/s = 30 \\
U_{wa} &: J/m^2/{}^\circ C/s = 0.2 \\
U_{ro} &: J/m^2/{}^\circ C/s = 0.15 \\
U_{wi}^{open} &: J/m^2/{}^\circ C/s = 10 \\
U_{wi}^{closed} &: J/m^2/{}^\circ C/s = 1.2
\end{aligned}
$$

4.3.4 Discrete Behaviour

Discrete behaviour means that the state changes happen only at distinct time points. Therefore, for discrete behaviour, a discrete time domain is sufficient. Discrete and continuous behaviour can be combined, leading to so-called combined systems. Such a combination needs a continuous time domain and must be done carefully (see [19]).

The best way to describe discrete state changes is state machines, sometimes called state charts [14]. A deterministic finite-state machine (DFSM) is given by a finite number of states including an initial state and transitions between these states. The DFSM is always in one of the states. The transitions can change the current state in response to external or internal triggers. It is possible to include actions when entering or leaving states. There are many possible extensions of simple DFSM, for example, actions for transitions. DFSMs are a natural abstraction of many modern devices like vending machines, elevators, traffic lights and combination locks.

SysML has a traditional graphical notation for DFSM using boxes with round corners for states and arrows for transitions. We present only a small selection of the possible DFSM constructs of SysML. SLX and Python provide libraries to present DFSM. The Python and SLX versions are textual.

Natural π	SysML
The DFSM has two states S1 and S2 and S1 is initial. At 12:00, S2 becomes active and on C, S1 becomes active. When entering S1, action A1 is executed; when exiting S2, A2 is executed. After 02:00 in S2, execution ends.	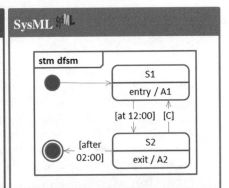

SLX	Python
| ```
dfsm Exa
   state S1 enter A1,
   state S2 leave A2,
   transitions
      S1 at 12:00     to S2,
      S2 with C       to S1,
      S2 after 02:00 to final
   initial S1;
``` | ```
class Exa(StateMachine):
   S1=State(initial=True)
   S2=State()
   F=State(final=True)
   at12=S1.to(S2)
   withC=S2.to(S1)
   after2=S2.to(F)
   def on_enter_S1(self): A1
   def on_exit_S2(self): A2
#calling at12 from outside:
exa=Exa(); exa.at12()
``` |

Charlie's Room—Episode 21: *Charlie's Schedule*

We can use a DFSM to describe the behaviour of Charlie (see Fig. 4.5).

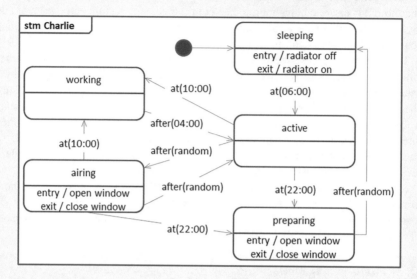

Fig. 4.5 Charlie's day

At night, Charlie is asleep. The morning routine begins at 6 and includes switching the radiator on (setting *room.r.isOn*). During the day, Charlie is active. Occasionally, the window is opened for a few minutes to get fresh air (setting *room.w.isOpen*). Charlie leaves for work at 10:00 and returns after four hours. At 22:00, the evening routine starts with opening the window. After a while, Charlie closes the window, switches off the radiator and goes to sleep. All the randomness in opening and closing the window is discussed in Sect. 4.3.5.

Alternatively, Charlie's behaviour can be captured in the table below.

Current state	Activity	Trigger	Next state
sleeping	entry: radiator off exit: radiator on	06:00	active
active		10:00	working
		22:00	preparing
		+ random$_1$	airing
working		+ 04:00	active
airing	entry: open window exit: close window	10:00	working
		22:00	preparing
		+ random$_2$	active
preparing	entry: open window exit: close window	+ random$_2$	sleeping

Another way to write the transition table is as follows:

from \ to	sleeping	active	working	airing	preparing
sleeping		06:00			
active			10:00	+ random$_1$	22:00
working		+ 04:00			
airing		+ random$_2$	10:00		22:00
preparing	+ random$_2$				

4.3.5 Random Behaviour

We have seen that Charlie's behaviour is not completely deterministic. There are several possible reasons for randomness in systems and models (see [19] and the case in Sect. 6.5).

- One reason could be that our focus does not consider all relevant attributes.
- Another reason could be our limited ability to measure the relevant attributes.
- Finally, randomness could be inherent in our worldview.

All of these reasons relate to uncertainty. Mathematics provides random variables, probabilities and probability distributions to quantify uncertainty (see [19, 25]). Uniform and normal distributions help to be precise about the expectations in the randomness (see Fig. 4.6). In a uniform distribution, all outcomes have an equal

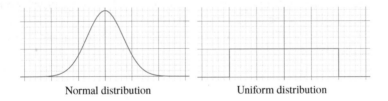

Normal distribution   Uniform distribution

Fig. 4.6 Normal and uniform probability distributions

probability of occurring within a specified range, for example, rolling a die. A normal distribution is symmetric around the average value (a bell-shaped curve), for example, the size of the human ear. Both have to be adjusted to the available precision. There are many other kinds of distributions. Which distribution is a good fit can be determined when we have data of actual outcomes (see again [19, 25]).

We can specify random attribute values by indicating the distribution with its parameters as follows:

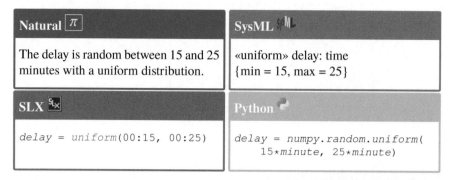

Natural π	SysML
The delay is random between 15 and 25 minutes with a uniform distribution.	«uniform» delay: time {min = 15, max = 25}

SLX
```
delay = uniform(00:15, 00:25)
```

Python
```
delay = numpy.random.uniform(
          15*minute, 25*minute)
```

Charlie's Room—Episode 22: *Random Behaviour*

In our example, opening and closing the window is a random event. Observations indicate that Charlie opens the window approximately every other hour with a standard deviation of 30 minutes (normal distribution). The window stays open for 5–10 minutes (uniform distribution). This can be described as follows:

```
randomOpen = normal(02:00, 00:30),
randomClose = uniform(00:05, 00:10)
```

The randomness of closing the window is caused by:

- The activity going on in the room while the window is open (not in our focus)
- The speed of the temperature drop, which depends on the current wind speed (not in our focus and difficult to measure)
- The subjective well-being of Charlie (inherently random in our world-view)

4.3.6 Collaborative Behaviour

There are three aspects of collaboration, sometimes named 3C of collaboration: communication, cooperation and coordination (see [5]). Communication means to exchange information, for example, by sending and receiving data. Cooperation means avoiding interference between objects, for example, sequentializing access to a printer. Coordination is based on a coordinator directing the actions of the objects. In our model, the objects collaborate using shared variables, so we do not present collaboration constructs here. Implicitly, our model is coordinated by creating and starting active objects, setting initial values and scheduling object activity.

Exercises

4.1 (Time) Consider a clock as a model of time.
When is a clock a correct model, and when is the model incorrect? How is this influenced by the perspective chosen?

4.2 (Architecture) Architectural drawings describe some aspects of buildings.
Sometimes, the drawing is prepared after the building is finished. Can we say that the building prescribed by the drawing is a model of the real building? Or is it the other way around?

4.3 (Discretization) Figure 4.4 shows how discrete data can be interpolated to form continuous data.
If we start with continuous data given by the cosine function, how can we extract discrete data at every full minute? How does the perspective influence the result?

4.4 (Darts) Dart throwing often has a considerable element of luck involved.
What are the reasons for these uncertainties? How could a change of perspective remove some of the randomness? How does the situation change if the player is a world champion?

References

1. Baader, F., Nipkow, T.: Term Rewriting and All That. Cambridge University Press, Cambridge (1999)
2. Beazley, D.M.: Python Essential Reference. Addison-Wesley Professional, Reading (2019)
3. Bjørner, D.: Domain Science and Engineering: A Foundation for Software Development. Springer Nature, Switzerland (2021)
4. Boman, M., Bubenko, J.A., Johannesson, P., Wangler, B.: Conceptual Modelling. Prentice Hall, London (1997)
5. Borghoff, U.M., Schlichter, J.H.: Computer-Supported Cooperative Work - Introduction to Distributed Applications. Springer, Berlin (2000)
6. Clements, P.C.: A survey of architecture description languages. In: Proceedings of the 8th International Workshop on Software Specification and Design, IWSSD '96, pp. 16–. IEEE Computer Society, Washington (1996). http://dl.acm.org/citation.cfm?id=857204.858261
7. Clewley, R.: PyDSTool: Python dynamical systems toolkit. https://github.com/robclewley/pydstool
8. Dahl, O.J., Myhrhaug, B., Nygård, K.: Simula 67. Common Base Language. Tech. rep., Norwegian Computing Center (1968)
9. Embley, D., Thalheim, B.: Handbook of Conceptual Modeling: Theory, Practice, and Research Challenges. Springer, Berlin (2012)
10. Friedenthal, S., Moore, A., Steiner, R.: A Practical Guide to SysML: The Systems Modeling Language. Morgan Kaufmann, Los Altos (2014)
11. Fritzson, P.: Introduction to Modeling and Simulation of Technical and Physical Systems with Modelica. Wiley, London (2006)
12. Gonzalez-Perez, C., Henderson-Sellers, B.: Metamodelling for Software Engineering. Wiley, London (2008)

13. Hahn, B., Valentine, D.T.: Essential MATLAB for Engineers and Scientists. Academic Press, New York (2017)
14. Harel, D., Politi, M.: Modeling Reactive Systems with Statecharts: The Statemate Approach. Computing McGraw-Hill. McGraw-Hill, New York (1998)
15. Henriksen, J.O.: Slx: the x is for extensibility [simulation software]. In: Simulation Conference, 2000. Proceedings. Winter, vol. 1, pp. 183–190 (2000). https://doi.org/10.1109/WSC.2000.899715
16. Karagiannis, D., Mayr, H.C., Mylopoulos, J. (eds.): Domain-Specific Conceptual Modeling, Concepts, Methods and Tools. Springer, Berlin (2016)
17. Klee, H., Allen, R.: Simulation of Dynamic Systems with MATLAB and Simulink. Taylor & Francis, CRC Press (2018)
18. Lamport, L.: Time, clocks, and the ordering of events in a distributed system. Commun. ACM 21(7), 558–565 (1978)
19. Lee, E.A.: Plato and the Nerd: The Creative Partnership of Humans and Technology. MIT Press, Cambridge (2017)
20. Muller, R.A.: Now: The Physics of Time. W. W. Norton & Company, New York (2016)
21. Murphy, G.L.: The Big Book of Concepts. MIT Press, Cambridge (2001)
22. Newton (anonymously), S.I.: Scala graduum caloris. calorum descriptiones & signa (newton's law of cooling). Philos. Trans. Roy. Soc. 22, 739–740 (1701)
23. Olivé, A.: Conceptual Modeling of Information Systems. Springer, Berlin (2007)
24. Rumpe, B.: Modeling with UML: Language, Concepts, Methods. Addison-Wesley Professional, Reading (2006)
25. Stirzaker, D.: Probability and Random Variables: A Beginner's Guide. Cambridge University Press, Cambridge (1999)
26. Tanenbaum, A.S., van Steen, M.: Distributed Systems: Principles and Paradigms. Pearson (2006)

Chapter 5
Programming

Programming today is a race between
software engineers striving to build
bigger and better idiot-proof programs,
and the Universe trying to produce
bigger and better idiots. So far, the
Universe is winning.

Rick Cook, *The Wizardry Compiled*

This chapter is devoted to programming, which is the creation of programs that prescribe systems. Therefore, Sect. 5.1 considers the connection between a program and its prescribed system. This means we discuss the semantics of descriptions related to snapshots and executions. We consider two main ways towards execution of a description, namely, compilation and interpretation. Section 5.2 explains how programming is used to develop new systems or new parts of existing systems without having a physical referent system as a basis. In Sect. 5.3, we look into the details of how the model descriptions as discussed in Chap. 4 are programmed. We look into the correctness of programming in Sect. 5.4, which is closely related to the correctness of models as discussed in Sect. 3.2. Finally, we explain where to find extra companion resources for this book in Sect. 5.5.

5.1 Definition of Programming

Modelling as discussed in Chap. 3 is typically used for understanding existing systems (see again Sect. 3.1). *Programming* is concerned with creating new systems which makes programming a creative activity, sometimes even considered an art [4, 21]. Programming is normally used in system development to create digital systems (see [9]). The same approach works for all kinds of created systems.

Most digital systems do not only contain new software but connect to existing systems and hardware and are operated by existing persons. They are embedded

© The Author(s), under exclusive license to Springer Nature Switzerland AG 2025
A. Prinz et al., *Understanding Modelling and Programming*,
https://doi.org/10.1007/978-3-031-71280-7_5

systems, combining existing parts with new parts to provide required functionalities as discussed in Sect. 2.2 and exemplified in the cases in Sects. 6.1 and 6.2. In [11] and [30], it is therefore emphasized that modelling and programming should be combined in system development. This requires a language that provides all the needed constructs, in particular the constructs presented in Chap. 4.

The relation between modelling and programming is best explained in Fig. 5.1, which is adapted from Fig. 3.2 and [11]. When we focus on the horizontal arrow,

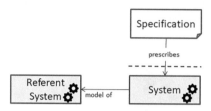

Fig. 5.1 Modelling and programming (Adapted from [11])

we handle existing systems and call it modelling. The referent system in this case is typically a physical system. It is the core of science. We discuss it in Sects. 5.3 and 5.4.

When we focus on the vertical arrow, we create new systems and call it programming. The referent system in this case is mental. This is the core of engineering; we discuss it in Sect. 5.2.

In both cases, a specification prescribes a system, which then is a model of a referent system. Programmers typically call their specifications 'code' or 'program'. We continue to use the term 'specification' for all precise descriptions that prescribe a system. Therefore, we define programming[1] as the production of specifications.

Definition 5.1 (Programming) *Programming* is the act or process of creating specifications to prescribe systems for a given purpose.

Since the referent system in programming is mental, it is often considered as the model of the planned system (see Fig. 5.2). Reversing the model-of relationship is

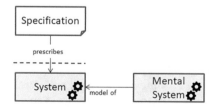

Fig. 5.2 The plan can be seen as a mental model of the planned system (Adapted from [11])

---

[1] An alternative term for 'programming' is 'implementation'.

possible because the central part of model-of is similarity, which is symmetric. With this view, science creates models for systems (Fig. 5.1), while engineering creates systems for models (Fig. 5.2) (see also [27]). In our view, the referent system came first and we prefer Fig. 5.1 instead of Fig. 5.2.

Programming relies on executable specifications, i.e. descriptions that are precise and executable. Executability means that some physical reality brings the specification to life, as indicated in [18] and defined in Sect. 5.1.3. This way, we can experiment early with the planned systems such that the specifications tend to become more down-to-earth and pragmatic (see [20]).

Section 5.1.1 explores the 'prescribes' relationship as the core of programming and introduces the concept of *runtime*. We discuss snapshots and runs in Sect. 5.1.2. Finally, Section 5.1.3 examines compilers and interpreters as actual tools for execution.

5.1.1 Languages and Semantics

Figure 5.3 shows that a system description (specification) prescribes a system, capturing the purpose part of our perspective. The specification and the prescribed system depend on the language used because a language is a set of descriptions with their semantics (Definition 4.1). This way, a language restricts what we can express, capturing the worldview.

Systems are sets of executions (Definition 2.2), and executions are time-ordered collections of snapshots (Definition 2.4). A snapshot is an object configuration with attribute values (Definition 2.3). This means that the specification prescribes the structure of snapshots (system states) and the possible system state changes.

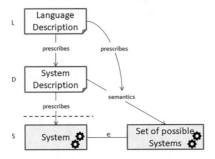

Fig. 5.3 Language, semantics and instantiation (Adapted from [34])

The specification semantics is a collection of possible systems (Definition 4.2). The system prescribed by the specification is one of those possible systems. In real system development, a system specification consists of several partial specifications prescribing different aspects of the system.

Figure 5.3 distinguishes three layers: the language layer L, the description layer D and the system layer S (see also Fig. 5.4, column LDS1). Remember that each upper layer contains descriptions (meta) of the next lower layer.

Layer	OMG	Room Example	LDS1	LDS2
metalanguage descriptions	M3	grammar language description		L
language descriptions	M2	SLX language description	L	D
system descriptions	M1	room SLX description	D	S
systems including models	M0	room system	S	

Fig. 5.4 Four layers of descriptions and systems, extended from Fig. 4.1

The same situation is repeated in the layers above (LDS2 and maybe even LDS3) as follows. The metalanguage description (now layer L) prescribes the metalanguage semantics, which maps the language description (now layer D) to a set of possible system specifications (not shown in Fig. 5.3). The system specification (now layer S) is one of those, such that the language description prescribes the system specification. The system specification in role S is dynamic: It can be changed by editors or similar tools. When the specification is in role D, it cannot be changed (see the discussion of runtime and specification time in Sect. 5.1.2).

A metalanguage is a description of descriptions (meta of meta) detailing the elements and semantics of descriptions. It should not be confused with a description of classification (meta of objects) as introduced in Sect. 4.2.2, which describes relationships between classes. Descriptions cross the layer boundary with 'prescribes', while classification stays on the same layer.

Language descriptions commonly feature the aspects structure, syntax and semantics [33] (see Fig. 5.5).

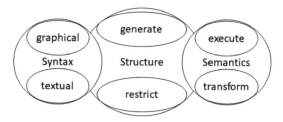

Fig. 5.5 Language aspects (Adapted from [33, 35])

Language *structure* defines the concepts of the language and their relations to each other (containment, reference, etc.), similar to the concepts of a system description. In other words, the structure aspect *generates* all possible specifications. In addition, constraints *restrict* the possible specifications by rejecting some of them as invalid.

Language (concrete) *syntax* provides a way to present a specification to its users. There can be different kinds of concrete syntax, e.g. *textual*, *graphical* or a combination of both (see also [6]).

Language *semantics* defines which systems are prescribed by a specification, given as a compiler (transform) or an interpreter (execute) (see Sect. 5.1.3). Please remember the difference between semantics and meaning (see Sect. 3.2.4). A precise language provides unambiguous semantics to all its specifications, supporting the justification of model correctness. Otherwise, the semantics may vary depending on the person or tool doing the prescription. In this book, precise languages are mathematics (formulae and function diagrams) and programming languages.

5.1.2 Runtime: Snapshots and Runs

We have established that a specification prescribes the structure of snapshots (system states; see Definition 2.3) and the possible system state changes. When we want to *create* executions incrementally and not only observe them, we need more information in the snapshots. An extended snapshot is called runtime state (RTS), while the runtime state changes are called execution behaviour or dynamic semantics.

It is common to distinguish between *specification time* ('the time of definition') and *runtime* ('the time of use'). Specification (description) time is related to the specification: its creation and adaptation. Runtime is related to the execution and the RTS. At runtime, the specification is considered fixed and is used.

The RTS is defined by the language used. The specification may contain several kinds of entities, for example, classes, attributes, differential equations, value tables and state machines. All of them can lead to different kinds of objects and values at runtime. The following elements are typical members of the RTS (see also [36]):

- The *specification* itself is available in the RTS so the execution can read from it.
- *Language-dependent RTS elements* are independent of the specification, e.g. predefined libraries, inputs from the environment (outside the system), model time (see Sect. 4.3.1) and the current activity of the program (program counter).
- *Specification-dependent RTS elements* are prescribed by parts of the specification, like attributes, objects, next activity and next activation time. This is the system state (Definition 2.3). Some specification elements do not prescribe elements in the RTS.

Charlie's Room—Episode 23: *RTS*

For the room, we find the following RTS elements.

- The room specification itself is present in the RTS.
- Language-dependent RTS elements are the clock for the model time and the current state of Charlie's DFSM.
- The specification-dependent RTS elements of a snapshot of Charlie's room have been described in Episode 4, for example, the value of the room temperature *room.temperature* = 20 °C. These values were also presented in graphical SysML in Fig. 4.2. Several specification parts do not prescribe any RTS element, for example, the formula to compute the volume in Episode 19 (simplified here): $V = l \cdot b \cdot \frac{h_{top} + h_{low}}{2}$. The computed value is part of the RTS, but the formula does not prescribe other RTS elements.

We observe RTS snapshots using our perspective, given by the language used. However, they are created in some reality, called realization. In a way, realization is the opposite of perspective because perspective reduces reality to a system and realization extends a system to reality. Often, several layers of realization are used on top of each other as indicated in Fig. 5.6 (see also [27]). The snapshot is shown as

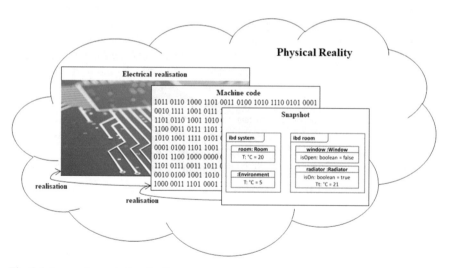

Fig. 5.6 Layers of snapshot realization

introduced in Sect. 4.2.1. First, it is realized using machine code, which is a lower-level perspective of the things going on in a computer. The realization of machine code can be electronics, which is another perspective. All these perspectives relate to the same underlying reality, shown as a cloud. Each realization layer is hardware for the next higher layer and software of the next lower layer. For each new lower layer of realization, additional information for its perspective must be added, commonly called deployment.

RTS snapshots allow the specification of RTS state changes (see [38]), which again allows attaching snapshots to time points (Sect. 4.3.1) to form executions (Definition 2.4). Executions are defined in the language semantics as detailed in [17]. The formal language semantics definitions of SDL in [16] and Java in [2] provide examples of how a language semantics definition might look. We discuss language semantics descriptions in Sect. 5.1.3.

Observing a run means observing a selected finite amount of snapshots, typically without the added RTS part. Alternatively, we can track system attribute values as graphs, representing the complete execution.

Charlie's Room—Episode 24: *Room Execution*

We observe an execution of Charlie's room model and track the relevant values in the diagram in Fig. 5.7.

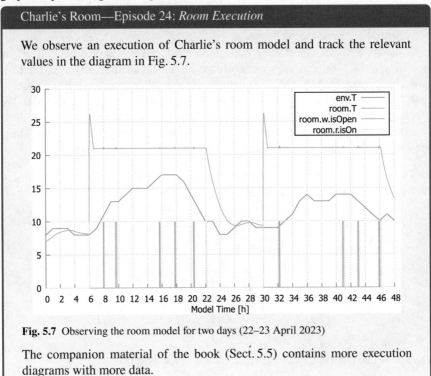

Fig. 5.7 Observing the room model for two days (22–23 April 2023)

The companion material of the book (Sect. 5.5) contains more execution diagrams with more data.

5.1.3 Interpreters and Compilers

As discussed in Sect. 5.1.2, a specification needs a reality that 'brings it to life', creating and assembling the needed RTS snapshots as prescribed by the language.

Definition 5.2 (Machine) A *machine* is an entity that executes a specification.

Fig. 5.8 A machine can execute a specification

Figure 5.8 shows a machine as a trapezoid containing the name of its native machine language (ML), whose specifications it can execute. A specification is a flipped trapezoid containing the name of the specification (Spec) and in which language it is written (ML). The combination of the machine and the specification is the prescribed system. We call a language and its specifications 'executable' if there is a (virtual) machine for the language.

A machine works well if the specification is written in machine language. This is often not the case, and the specification is written in another language, say L. L could be Python, SLX, SysML, mathematics or any other specification language.

If Spec is written in L, we have two ways to execute it on the machine ML. We can adapt the machine or the specification. Adapting the machine is done with an interpreter (see [36]) and adapting the specification with a compiler (see [1]). These are also the two main ways of describing the language semantics (see [17]).

Definition 5.3 (Interpreter) An *interpreter* is a specification (a program) describing how to read and execute a specification in a language L.

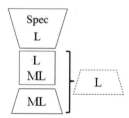

Fig. 5.9 An interpreter specifies how to read and execute specifications

Figure 5.9 shows an interpreter as a square containing the language it understands (L) and the language it is written in (ML). An interpreter is a specification and not a system. It has to run to become a system. A simple form of an interpreter is a language extension of ML by libraries or syntax extensions (see [19]). Because the L interpreter is written in ML, it can be executed by the machine ML, which allows Spec written in L to be executed on top of the two. Interpreters can be stacked on top of each other leading to realization layers as shown in Fig. 5.6, changing perspective for each layer. As an example, the machine code is interpreted by the electronics.

The combination of an interpreter with a machine forms a *virtual machine*, i.e. a running interpreter. Figure 5.9 shows how the interpreter L-ML and the machine ML form the virtual machine L². A virtual machine works like a real machine (Fig. 5.8).

Definition 5.4 (Compiler) A *compiler* is a specification (a program) describing how to translate a specification in a language L to a semantically equivalent specification in another language ML.

A compiler is used at specification time, sometimes called 'compile time'. Like an interpreter, a compiler has to run to become a system. The compiler itself (depicted as the T-symbol in Fig. 5.10) is also written in a language; for simplicity, we assume it is written in ML, such that it is executable on ML. The compiler does not execute

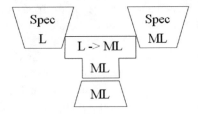

Fig. 5.10 A compiler translates a specification from one language to another

Spec (in L); it creates an equivalent specification Spec written in ML (see Sect. 5.4). The resulting Spec written in ML can be executed by machine ML (see Fig. 5.8).

Compilers are the core of system development with the model-driven development (MDD) method (see [26, 40]). In MDD, a high-level specification is translated stepwise into more and more low-level specifications until they reach a state where they can be executed on a machine.

5.2 Programming New System Parts

Most systems are embedded systems because they contain existing parts and new parts as discussed in Sect. 2.2 and shown in Fig. 5.11. The difference between new (grey) and existing (white) parts is not given in the specification but in the relations of the system parts to the parts of reality (Referent System) (see Fig. 5.1). We use programming for specifications of new parts and modelling for existing parts. As our perspective is object-oriented (see Fig. 2.2), we can use object-oriented methods of programming for digital systems (see [5]).

---

² A complete virtual machine often needs a *runtime environment (RTE)* comprising the interpreter, libraries and other infrastructure.

Charlie's Room—Episode 25: *Compilers and Interpreters*

Charlie wants to automate the handling of the heating using a home automation application. It should reduce the room temperature at night and switch off the heating when the window is open. This behaviour can be expressed with the following rules:

1. At 22:00, set the target temperature to 15 °C.
2. At 05:30, set the target temperature to 21 °C.
3. When the window is opened, switch off the heating.
4. When the window is closed, switch on the heating.

Let's assume that Charlie is Norwegian and does not understand the English rules above. Then Charlie can find a friend to translate the rules into Norwegian. The friend is now a running *compiler*, translating from English to Norwegian. Charlie is a *machine* for the resulting Norwegian specification because Charlie can execute the Norwegian rules.

Looking more closely, we see that many of the activities in the rules are complex. For example, setting the target temperature means dialling the new temperature by turning the knob at the heating. Detecting 22:00 means continuously monitoring the clock until it shows the longer hand at 12 and the shorter hand at 10.

This way, Charlie is also a running *interpreter* of the language based on simpler machine code built into Charlie. We could even go deeper and consider the smaller mental and physical activities needed, thereby creating a similar layering as indicated in Fig. 5.6.

When programming new parts of a system, it is important to be able to use the new parts together with the old parts. This can be easy when the old parts have digital models, but it is more tricky when the old parts are regular physical devices.

There are two ways to use a combined specification as shown in Fig. 5.12. The specifications of the existing parts can be used to create a simulation of those parts for virtual experiments with the new parts. This is indicated at the left in Fig. 5.12. All the existing entities are simulated and executed together with the new entities. After

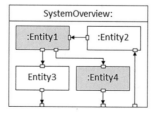

Fig. 5.11 Systems consist of new (grey) and existing (white) parts (Adapted from [11])

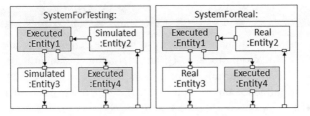

Fig. 5.12 Simulating or running the specification (Adapted from [11])

finishing the simulated tests of the new entities, the same entities can be connected to the real existing entities as shown to the right in Fig. 5.12. This is the final application scenario. If the models of the existing entities are correct, then the new entities work as expected in the real application (see also digital twins in Sect. 3.1). Examples of that approach are shown in the cases in Sects. 6.1 and 6.2.

5.3 Programming Existing Formal Specifications

Modelling leads to a formal specification that prescribes the (model) system we are interested in. Often, such model specification is created by domain experts with their view of formality, using (formal) domain-specific modelling [22]. Writing a specification in a way that is understandable for humans is also known in programming as literate programming [23], language-oriented programming [8] and domain-specific languages (DSLs) [13][3]. In the domain, there is agreement that the DSL is the right way to express things, but there is no machine available to execute the DSL specifications.

In this situation, a programmer can be asked to translate the specification to a language that does have a machine, thereby acting as a human compiler. This means the programmer needs to understand the DSL, read the specification written in the DSL, be fluent in the intended programming language and write the original specification in the programming language. It is even better if the translation is automatic as in the case in Sect. 6.3, where a DSL for social simulation is translated to an executable language.

For the translation, it is an advantage to find a target language that is similar to the language we start with. For the mathematical constructs we have discussed in Chap. 3, the language SLX (Simulation Language with eXtensibility) [19] is a good match because it allows to express time-continuous, time-discrete and random behaviour. As discussed in Sect. 4.1, SysML [14] and Python [3] are other good candidates.

---

[3] Sometimes, the term 'pseudo-code' is used instead of DSL.

Charlie's Room—Episode 26: *Adding a KNX Controller*

Charlie wants to automatically regulate the temperature using a controller based on the KNX protocol [24], an international standard for building automation. Before starting with the work, Charlie wants to know how the change will influence the room temperature, making experiments with the model. This can ensure that the controller controls the room temperature correctly. The controller code used in the simulation can then be re-used for the real controller as part of the deployment.

The controller is added to the other elements of the room system (Fig. 3.3) as shown in Fig. 5.13.

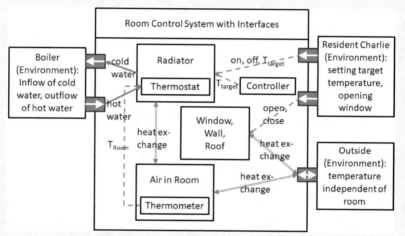

Fig. 5.13 KNX target temperature controller

The rules for controlling the radiator target temperature (*room.r.Tt*) are currently given in English in Episode 25. Charlie must translate them into a language that the controller understands, thereby being a human compiler. A simple language for controller programming is IFTTT (*IF This Then That*) [31] helping to connect triggers to actions. Both triggers and actions come from KNX devices. Each device announces the triggers (available information) and the actions it provides.

Charlie's thermostat is equipped with KNX and has an action to set the target temperature and a trigger to read the current room temperature. Charlie wants to switch on the radiator early in the morning, such that the room is warm when leaving the bed. Similarly, the radiator can be turned off automatically in the evening to avoid forgetting it. This could lead to the following two IFTTT statements (see also Episode 25):

IF it is past 05:30 THEN set room.r.tT to 21 °C.

IF it is past 22:00 THEN set room.r.tT to 15 °C.

Moreover, the thermostat room temperature sensor could be used to program the thermostat control as described in Episode 14 directly into the controller.

The language SLX provides similar basic concepts as the language Simula-67 [7] (i.e. its standard library 'simulation') using a syntax similar to the language C++ [41]. A particular strength of SLX is the runtime efficiency of its simulator core functions and the possibility of expanding the language in its grammar with domain-specific expressions and instructions. SLX supports continuous behaviour with a library module *continuous*, supporting ordinary differential equations. Various methods for numerical integration are available (see also Sect. 5.4.2).

Charlie's Room—Episode 27: *Programming the Room Model*

The model of Charlie's room is currently given in mathematics and SysML. We want to express it in SLX. The SLX specification is structurally equivalent to the structure description given in Figs. 4.2 and 4.3. Here, we only present parts of the specification, the complete code can be found in the companion material as explained in Sect. 5.5. The room components as presented in Episode 17 are defined as objects of classes.

```
pointer (Environment)    env;
pointer (Room)           room;
pointer (Resident)       charlie;

passive class Environment implements (Behavior) { ...
  pointer (Boiler) b; ...
}
passive class Room() implements (Behavior) { ...
  pointer (Window) w;
  pointer (Radiator) r; ...
}
```

- *env* as an object of *Environment* simulates the outside temperature.
- *room* as an object of *Room* determines the room temperature based on the heat flow considering radiator, walls, window and roof.
- *charlie* as an object of *Resident* sets the target temperature and opens and closes the window.
- *b* as an object of *Boiler* determines the temperature of the water boiler.
- *w* as an object of *Window* can be opened and closed.
- *r* as an object of *Radiator* determines the time-dependent radiator temperature and keeps the target temperature.

The *main* program is a concurrent execution in SLX, starting and stopping the system. At start, all required objects are created and started, including an object *theIntegrator* that is responsible for handling the differential equations. The system stops after the experiment duration, e.g. after 2 days of model time. The *main* program only activates (starts) objects of active classes.

```
procedure main {
  theIntegrator= new RKM_Integrator (...);
  env= new Environment;    // also creates b
  room= new Room;          // also creates r and w
  charlie= new Resident;
  ...
  activate charlie;
  activate theIntegrator;
  ...
  wait until time >= EXPERIMENT_DURATION;
  exit(0); // stop
}
```

The differential equations for the room introduced in Episode 20 are written
in SLX syntax as follows:

```
concrete method derivatives(double t) {
  double Q_R_Rate = r->U * r->A * (r->T.state - T.state);
  double Q_wiRate = w->U * w->A * (T.state - env->T.state);
  double Q_waRate = U_wa * A_wa * (T.state - env->T.state);
  double Q_roRate = U_ro * A_ro * (T.state - env->T.state);
  T.rate = (Q_R_Rate - Q_wiRate - Q_waRate - Q_roRate) /
           (V * D_air * C_air);
}
```

When modelling window heat loss, the coefficient U_wi depends on the
closed or open window, which again is set by *charlie*.

In the method *derivatives*, we can access the current value of a variable v
using $v.state$, while the current change of that variable is denoted $v.rate$. In
mathematics, this would be $v(t)$ and $v'(t)$. The time parameter t is not written
due to syntactic simplifications of the function handling.

Room constants as introduced in Episode 2, 19 and 20 are expressed in SLX
as follows:

```
constant double h_top  = 3.7;
constant double h_low  = 0.7;
constant double b      = 6.0;
constant double l      = 4.0;
constant double V      = l*b*(h_low+h_top)/2;
constant double A_ro   = 2*l*sqrt(2)*(h_top-h_low);
constant double U_ro   = 0.15 / Second;
```

The *Resident* class is active. Its activity is described by a DFSM as shown
in Episode 21 including random behaviour as described in Episode 22. The
DFSM is called in the *actions* method of Resident. Here, we only show
the state *airing*. The full code can be found in the companion material as
explained in Sect. 5.5.

```
dfsm Charlie
  state airing
    enter room->w->isOpen = TRUE
    leave room->w->isOpen = FALSE,
  ...
  transitions
    airing    at 10:00 to working,
    airing    with randomClose to active,
    airing    at 22:00 to preparingNight,
  ...
  where
    randomClose = uniform(00:05, 00:10)
  initial sleeping;

class Resident() { actions { ...
  run Charlie; // run the DFSM
} }
```

5.4 Correct Programs

For programming, the same correctness considerations as for modelling apply (see Sect. 3.2), where we considered *validation* and *verification*. In addition, we also consider *compilation*. All three approaches are combined in the tool ARCTIS [25].

- *Compilation* allows to translate a high-level system description into an executable system specification which (by definition) has the same behaviour as the original description. This approach is called correctness by construction. However, the compiled code is only correct if the compiler is correct. The correctness of a compiler can be checked against the language description using verification. The case in Sect. 6.3 is based on compilation.
- *Verification* is the comparison of two descriptions by way of their semantics, for example, a requirements specification and a design description, or high-level code and low-level code. Both descriptions are formal, and there are mathematical methods that allow comparison (see, e.g. [43]). Please note that the same approach can also be used for comparing generated code with the original description if a higher level of correctness is needed than trusting the compiler. Verification is used in Sects. 5.4.1 and 5.4.2.
- *Testing* is a special case of validation, describing the process of exemplifying correctness by comparing the results of experiments (the tests) between the tested system and the referent system. For programming, the referent system is mental: the plan or intention. A test plan can ensure that the tests together cover the range of expected behaviour. In test theory, several coverage criteria are used [10]. Testing does not provide a complete match between the two compared specifications,

as the number of possible experiments is typically infinite, and testing can only check a finite and even very small number of them. The case in Sect. 6.2 uses testing for an embedded system.

The descriptions of the models in Chap. 3 are given in established mathematical formalisms and notations. However, when we want to build running models out of these descriptions, we must realize the mathematical concepts in a program and verify correctness. We will look into the programming of random numbers (Sect. 5.4.1), differential equations (Sect. 5.4.2) and concurrency (Sect. 5.4.3).

5.4.1 Programming Random Numbers

In Sect. 4.3.5, probability distributions were introduced in case there is not enough deterministic information for the desired system effect. Then, the effect is captured with a random number. The random number is close enough to the original effect if it has a similar distribution in the perspective used. Random number generators often provide a uniform distribution, while other distributions can be created using established methods [12].

There are two general ways to produce random numbers: real random numbers and pseudo-random numbers. Real random numbers rely on real random events in the current perspective. A common example is using real time with sufficient precision (e.g. milliseconds). The last digits of the time are typically random with a uniform distribution.

Pseudo-random numbers [15] are deterministic sequences of numbers with verified statistical characteristics matching real, random numbers. The next number is calculated from the current number using a deterministic formula. Pseudo-random number generators start with a seed value such that the calculation yields the same sequence of random numbers. Changing the seed value will produce a different random sequence. Pseudo-random numbers offer the advantage that experiments can be repeated using the same seed value such that different people can get the same results. In addition, it also allows tracking of errors when the system does not work as expected.

5.4.2 Programming Differential Equations

The programming and simulation of combined systems containing both time-continuous and time-discrete executions are challenging due to their different handling of time (see Sect. 4.3.1 and [27]). Usual computers are digital, meaning that they are based on discrete mathematics [37], basically handling natural numbers. They can handle discrete behaviour with discrete time but fail to handle continuous behaviour with continuous time, which is based on continuous mathematics (real numbers) [39]. Continuous behaviour is better handled using analog computers [42], which again are not able to cover discrete behaviour. Our systems consist of both kinds of behaviour, and this poses a challenge.

Due to the overwhelming majority of computers being digital, we want to handle continuous behaviour and their differential equations in a digital (discrete) world. For this purpose, we approximate values and replace continuous time with sufficiently small discrete time steps that align with our precision requirements for the data. The programming of differential equations is the subject of numerical mathematics [32]. Numerical mathematics does not solve the mathematical equations analytically but rather approximates them using rational numbers with verified approximation methods like the Euler forward and backward methods, as well as the Runge-Kutta-Fehlberg method (see [32]). The *continuous* library of SLX provides such methods including adaptive interval handling.

It is possible to get a high precision using these methods, but not infinite as would be the case for true reals. Therefore, utmost care must be taken that the results of a numerical calculation are faithful to its original mathematical description. There are two main problems when using digital methods for analogue phenomena. First, the precision is not good enough, and second, the errors add up too much.

Due to their limited precision, the result of a computation with approximated rational numbers differs from the same computation with the precise real numbers. We hope that small differences in the input precision lead to small differences in the output (computation) precision such that the overall precision is within the acceptable limits of our perspective. This is often the case, but in so-called chaotic systems [28], small changes in the input lead to huge changes in the output. Fortunately, many functions are stable with respect to small changes, and numerical methods can detect problems in many cases.

When computing differential equations, the cumulative error problem appears because the calculation of the function value for the next model time point uses the calculated function value of the previous model time point. This means it starts with an approximate value, thus leading to a cascade of approximations that finally can exceed our precision limits. Fortunately, it is possible to estimate the error in the calculation, such that we can ensure that the error is below the limits of our perspective. Many kinds of differential equations are also self-correcting in that the accuracy error gets less than the precision in the input.

5.4.3 Programming Concurrency

The objects in our models work concurrently and are typically synchronized based on model time. In the execution, they work independently until they need to interact with each other. The interaction of their continuous behaviour was discussed in Sect. 5.4.2, and the continuous steps must be aligned with the discrete steps. Because the objects work independently and are not dependent on real time, they can execute one after the other, instead of concurrently. This is called *interleaving*.

For interleaving, the activities of the objects are executed in some order. This is done with *scheduling* (see also Sect. 4.3.6). Scheduling has to make sure that the system does not lock itself. Objects are sorted according to their activity status for scheduling. In SLX, the following states are possible:

- A *moving* object is active or waits for execution. The time of the object is the current model time.
- A *scheduled* object is delayed by a defined duration. After that, it becomes moving.
- An object is *waiting* if it is suspended without a deadline. It can be activated by another object and then become moving again.
- *Terminated* objects have finished their active life and are now passive and readable.

Scheduling and interleaving are known methods (see [29]) to handle concurrency on the same machine and are available on any modern computer, for example, when showing several computer windows in parallel.

5.5 Companion Material

The book provides one example of modelling and programming, namely, Charlie's room. In the book preparation, SLX and Python tools were used to work with this example. All the code is available to readers who want to see more details or play with the models.

For this book, the companion material is provided in GitHub at the address `https://prinzandreas.github.io/ModellingProgramming/`.

The following elements are available in the companion material.

- The room model specification in SLX.
- The room model specification in Python.
- The SLX tool (student version).
- Plots of room simulations.
- Several SysML diagrams of Charlie's room.

In addition, more material is added on the fly, such as hints for solutions to the exercises.

Exercises

5.1 (Synchronized Traffic Lights) A city wants to reprogram the traffic lights to avoid traffic jams. The new programs should be tested in a model before deployment. What perspective do you propose for the model to capture all relevant elements? What are the RTS elements, and how do they relate to the three categories of RTS elements?

5.2 (Compilers and Interpreters) Suppose we have a machine understanding ML and a compiler written in ML translating SLX to ML.
Can we use the SLX compiler and the ML machine to create a (virtual) SLX machine, thereby making SLX executable?

5.3 (Testing) Testing is a way to validate a new system. A number of tests are run in the mental original and in the new system, and the results are compared.
Which methods would you propose to test a new chair? Which tests should be selected?

5.4 (Random Numbers) Pseudo-random numbers are a realization of real random numbers.
How could you verify or validate that they are correct?

References

1. Aho, A.V., Sethi, R., Ullman, J.D.: Compilers: Principles, Techniques, and Tools. Addison-Wesley Longman Publishing, Boston (1986)
2. Alves-Foss, J. (ed.): Formal Syntax and Semantics of Java. Lecture Notes in Computer Science. Springer, Berlin (1999)
3. Beazley, D.M.: Python Essential Reference. Addison-Wesley Professional, Reading (2019)
4. Bentley, J.: Programming Pearls, 2nd edn. Addison–Wesley, Boston (1999)
5. Booch, G., Maksimchuk, R.A., Engle, M.W., Young, B.J., Conallen, J.: Object-Oriented Analysis and Design with Applications. Addison-Wesley Professional, Reading (2007)
6. Chomsky, N.: Lectures on Government and Binding - The Pisa Lectures. Mouton, De Gruyter (1993)
7. Dahl, O.J., Myhrhaug, B., Nygård, K.: Simula 67. common base language. Tech. rep., Norwegian Computing Center (1968)
8. Dmitriev, S.: Language oriented programming: The next programming paradigm. JetBrains onBoard **1**(2) (2004). Accessed 30 May 2024
9. Endres, A., Rombach, D.: A Handbook of Software and Systems Engineering - Empirical Observations, Laws and Theories. Addison Wesley, Reading (2003)
10. Everett, G.D., McLeod Jr., R.: Software Testing: Testing Across the Entire Software Development Life Cycle. Wiley, London (2007)
11. Fischer, J., Møller-Pedersen, B., Prinz, A.: Modelling of systems for real. In: Proceedings of the 4th International Conference on Model-Driven Engineering and Software Development, pp. 427–434 (2016). https://doi.org/10.5220/0005825704270434
12. Forbes, C., Evans, M., Hastings, N., Peacock, B.: Statistical Distributions. John Wiley & Sons, London (2010)
13. Fowler, M.: Domain-Specific Languages. Addison-Wesley Professional, Reading (2010)
14. Friedenthal, S., Moore, A., Steiner, R.: A Practical Guide to SysML: The Systems Modeling Language. Morgan Kaufmann, Los Altos (2014)
15. Gentle, J.E.: Random Number Generation and Monte Carlo Methods. Springer, Berlin (2003)
16. Glässer, U., Gotzhein, R., Prinz, A.: The formal semantics of SDL-2000: Status and perspectives. Comput. Netw. **42**(3), 343–358 (2003). https://doi.org/10.1016/S1389-1286(03)00247-0
17. Gunter, C.A.: Semantics of Programming Languages: Structures and Techniques. MIT Press, Cambridge (1992)
18. Harel, D., Marelly, R.: Come, Let's Play, Scenario-Based Programming Using LSCs and the Play-Engine. Springer, Berlin (2003)

19. Henriksen, J.O.: SLX: the x is for extensibility [simulation software]. In: Simulation Conference, 2000. Proceedings. Winter, vol. 1, pp. 183–190 vol.1 (2000). https://doi.org/10.1109/WSC.2000.899715

20. Hunt, A., Thomas, D.: The Pragmatic Programmer: Your Journey to Mastery. Addison-Wesley Professional, Reading (1999)

21. Jackson, M.: Problem Frames: Analysing and Structuring Software Development Problems. Pearson Education, Harlowe (2007)

22. Kelly, S., Tolvanen, J.: Domain-Specific Modeling - Enabling Full Code Generation. Wiley, London (2008)

23. Knuth, D.E.: Literate Programming. No. 27 in CSLI Lecture Notes. Center for the Study of Language and Information at Stanford/California (1992)

24. KNX Association: KNX Handbook for Home and Building Control. KNX Association (2021)

25. Kraemer, F.A., Slåtten, V., Herrmann, P.: Tool Support for the Rapid Composition, Analysis and Implementation of Reactive Services. J. Syst. Softw. **82**(12), 2068–2080 (2009)

26. Krogstie, J.: Model-Based Development and Evolution of Information Systems. Springer, Berlin (2012)

27. Lee, E.A.: Plato and the Nerd: The Creative Partnership of Humans and Technology. MIT Press, Cambridge (2017)

28. Lorenz, E.: The Essence of Chaos. Jessie and John Danz Lectures. Taylor & Francis, London (1995)

29. Lynch, N.A.: Distributed Algorithms. Morgan Kaufmann Publishers, San Francisco (1996)

30. Madsen, O.L., Møller-Pedersen, B.: A unified approach to modeling and programming. In: Proceedings of the 13th International Conference on Model Driven Engineering Languages and Systems: Part I, MODELS'10, pp. 1–15. Springer, Berlin (2010)

31. Martinez, A.: The Ultimate IFTTT Guide: Use The Web's Most Powerful Tool Like A Pro. Amazon Media (2013). https://www.amazon.co.uk/Ultimate-IFTTT-Guide-Webs-Powerful-ebook/dp/B00FK1X1YQ

32. Press, W.H., Teukolsky, S.A., Vetterling, W.T., Flannery, B.P.: Numerical Recipes: The Art of Scientific Computing. Cambridge University Press, Cambridge (2007)

33. Prinz, A.: Teaching Language Engineering Using MPS, pp. 315–336. Springer, Cham (2021). https://doi.org/10.1007/978-3-030-73758-0_11

34. Prinz, A., Engebretsen, M., Gjøsæter, T., Møller-Pedersen, B., Xanthopoulou, T.D.: Models, systems, and descriptions. Front. Comput. Sci. **5** (2023). https://doi.org/10.3389/fcomp.2023.1031807

35. Prinz, A., Møller-Pedersen, B., Fischer, J.: Modelling and testing of real systems. In: Leveraging Applications of Formal Methods, Verification and Validation: Discussion, Dissemination, Applications - 7th International Symposium, ISoLA 2016, Imperial, Corfu, Greece, October 10–14, 2016, Proceedings, Part II, pp. 119–130 (2016). https://doi.org/10.1007/978-3-319-47169-3_9

36. Prinz, A., Møller-Pedersen, B., Fischer, J.: Object-oriented operational semantics. In: Proceedings of SAM 2016, LNCS 9959. Springer, Berlin (2016)

37. Rosen, K.H.: Discrete Mathematics and its Applications. McGraw-Hill, New York (2018)

38. Scheidgen, M., Fischer, J.: Human Comprehensible and Machine Processable Specifications of Operational Semantics, pp. 157–171. Springer, Berlin (2007). https://doi.org/10.1007/978-3-540-72901-3_12

39. Spivak, M.: Calculus. Cambridge University Press, Cambridge (2008)

40. Stahl, T., Völter, M.: Model-Driven Software Development: Technology, Engineering, Management. Wiley, Chichester (2006)

41. Stroustrup, B.: The C++ Programming Language. Addison-Wesley Professional, Reading (2013)

42. Ulmann, B.: Analog Computing. De Gruyter Oldenbourg, Berlin, Boston (2022). https://doi.org/10.1515/9783110787740

43. Woodcock, J., Larsen, P.G., Bicarregui, J., Fitzgerald, J.: Formal methods: practice and experience. ACM Comput. Surv. **41**(4) (2009). https://doi.org/10.1145/1592434.1592436

Chapter 6
More Cases

> You never change things by fighting
> the existing reality. To change
> something, build a new model that
> makes the existing model obsolete.
>
> —————————————————————
>
> Buckminster Fuller

We have explored concepts and theories about modelling and programming using a small example. This is of course not enough to embrace the whole area of models. Therefore, this chapter provides several use cases of modelling and programming such that the concepts introduced in this book are shown in several contexts. For each case, we consider the perspective and related system, the model with its use and the programming involved. We start with two technological systems, one in the area of earthquake early warning (Sect. 6.1) and one in the area of offshore operations (Sect. 6.2). We continue with two cases in the area of social modelling concerning bullying (Sect. 6.3) and a pandemic (Sect. 6.4). Finally, we have two cases related to cultural heritage, one around the modelling of memorial tours (Sect. 6.5) and one about the restoration of a destroyed landmark (Sect. 6.6). All cases are described in other publications and can be considered in more detail.

6.1 Earthquake Early Warning

An earthquake is a natural phenomenon that occurs when there is a sudden release of tension in the Earth's crust, causing the ground to shake, often resulting in the shaking and displacement of buildings, structures and the Earth's surface. Earthquakes can vary in size and range from barely noticeable minor tremors to major events that can cause significant destruction and loss of life [25].

The energy is initially released at a point called *hypocentre*. The *epicentre* is the point at the ground directly above the hypocentre. From the hypocentre, waves of energy, called seismic waves, are released that travel through the Earth's crust in all

© The Author(s), under exclusive license to Springer Nature Switzerland AG 2025 75
A. Prinz et al., *Understanding Modelling and Programming*,
https://doi.org/10.1007/978-3-031-71280-7_6

directions. The seismic waves are responsible for the damage. They also allow us to find the earthquake's location, magnitude and depth. There are three main types of seismic waves: primary waves, secondary waves and surface waves.

- Primary waves (P-waves) are the fastest seismic waves (5–7 km/s). They compress and expand the rock in the same direction they travel, similar to sound waves through the air. Typically, P-waves do not cause much destruction.
- Secondary waves (S-waves) travel 1.7 times slower than P-waves (3–4 km/s). They move the ground perpendicular to the wave propagation direction. They cause considerable damage.
- Surface waves travel along the Earth's surface and are slower than P-waves and S-waves. They are responsible for the most significant damage during an earthquake.

With our current knowledge and technology, predicting an earthquake event is impossible. We can identify places with high tension, but the actual event of the release cannot be predicted. It is possible, however, to estimate the probability of an earthquake occurring based on the current tension.

We cannot predict earthquakes, but we can get an early warning for an earthquake in progress due to the time differences in the seismic waves. Depending on the distance to the hypocentre, a few seconds to some tens of minutes remain for an early warning (see also Fig. 6.1). Even a few seconds are often enough to protect critical infrastructure with an automatic shutdown.

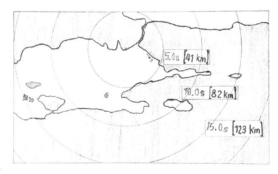

Fig. 6.1 Early warning times in the Istanbul area (©2024 Joachim Fischer, inspired by [8] – all rights reserved)

Seismic waves are detected using sensors called seismometers, which track the ground movement caused by these waves. Devices recording these measurements are referred to as seismographs. It is important to capture movements in various directions because different waves shake the earth in different ways.

An Earthquake Early Warning System (EEWS) relies on detecting P-waves before the slower and more damaging S-waves and surface waves [11]. The main aim of an EEWS is straightforward: to provide as much warning time as possible while minimizing the occurrence of false alarms and missed warnings.

This section explains the Self-Organizing Seismic Early Warning Information Network (SOSEWIN) [7, 8], which was developed within the EU-project SAFER (Seismic eArly warning For EuRope)[1]. SOSEWIN is an ad hoc sensor network with cooperating seismic sensor nodes. SAFER developed technology for real-time analysis of seismic signals and triggering actions like shutting down critical technical systems. It also supports rapid response decisions for emergency management.

6.1.1 Perspective

With the purpose of detecting earthquakes, we restrict our attention to detecting movements of the Earth with sensors and do not consider streets, buildings, trees and people. Seismometers (sensor nodes) are placed on the ground, and we can measure Earth's movements at these places. For the sensors, we are interested in their position (precision 100 meters), measuring capacity and connection to the other nodes. We ignore all the elements of reality outside the local context and even Earth's curvature. Even though there are reasons for the earthquake, we are less interested in those than in the location of the hypocentre. Depending on the seismometer placement, there might be noise from Earth's movements due to cars on the streets. We consider the communication delay of the nodes, but we ignore the execution time of the nodes, which is very small compared to the communication delay.

6.1.2 Programming and Descriptions

The success of the EEWS sensor network depends on the solution of a number of problems, namely, information exchange in the ad hoc sensor network, detection of an earthquake and handling of node failures. Earthquakes do not occur too often, and in case they do, we want the network to work well. Therefore, we cannot test in reality but need to test in a model. For these tests, we need a model of earthquakes (the existing part) and programs of the sensor nodes (the new parts).

The sensor nodes are programmed in C++, while the model simulation is done using the C++ library ODEM-X[2] and the network simulator ns-3[3] given as C++ library. This allows the creation of a virtual network of sensor nodes where we can run experiments with different kinds of earthquakes, both recorded and generated.

Expensive, high-precision seismometers help identify the occurrence of an earthquake precisely. However, they cannot be placed in densely populated areas, as the shaking of the ground from traffic disturbs them. Low-cost sensors with less pre-

---

[1] Seismic eArly warning For EuRope, https://cordis.europa.eu/project/id/36935

[2] https://sourceforge.net/projects/odemx/

[3] https://www.nsnam.org/

cision are used in SOSEWIN, achieving sufficient precision for early warning by combining several sensors to identify P-waves cooperatively.

A serious problem in earthquake detection is the damage caused by the earthquake. If the equipment installed for detection does not survive the seismic wave, it cannot issue a warning. Therefore, an early warning system is often composed of several independent sensors and processors capable of warning, connected to a network. Older EEWS use a centralized network of nodes (see [6]). A centralized network is simpler for the detection procedure, as all available data is routed to one place, but leads to problems if the central place is harmed by the earthquake.

In SOSEWIN [7], the network is decentralized and ad hoc, including local detection with a distributed decision algorithm. New nodes connect easily due to the ad hoc nature of the network as depicted in Fig. 6.2 (see also [8]). When the network is disrupted in an earthquake, the remaining nodes organize themselves quickly. This allows increasing the node density easily on the fly, fixing holes in the coverage due to broken or missing sensors or just increasing coverage in general. This can be essential for damage assessment and to help rescue teams communicate with victims.

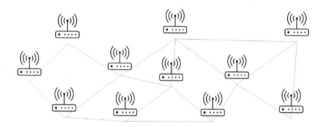

Fig. 6.2 Wireless sensor network

Therefore, in SOSEWIN, nodes must be programmed for sensing (monitoring earth movements using seismometer and GPS functionality), routing (forwarding of received messages in the sensor network by wireless communication), alerting (detecting earthquake patterns and issuing or resetting alarms) and management (organizing and managing the sensor network).

6.1.3 Earthquake Model

The geological theory of earthquakes is difficult and includes heavy equations from the fields of finite-strain theory describing the movement and intensity of seismic waves. The movement heavily depends on the characteristics of the different layers within the earth, and they only apply very locally. Using these formulas, we can calculate the predicted measurements of the seismometers, given their geographical position, the position of the hypocentre and the amount of stress released through the earthquake. Existing simulators [28, 35] can use these predictions to create 'artificial earthquakes'. Obviously, the description of the formulas in a simulator is a case of programming.

Such a simulator can provide snapshots of sensor readings as time series. The simulator takes a long time to calculate the correct scenario, but after that, the scenario can be replayed as often as needed. Alternatively, it is possible to record actual earthquakes and use this data for simulations. Unfortunately, it is very difficult to get a good-enough coverage of data from real earthquakes.

In our case, it is not important how we get access to earthquake data, because the interesting questions are related to the detection of earthquakes and the possibility of early warning. This can be done based on any set of earthquake data that can be broken down to the positions of our sensor nodes. A mixture of prerecorded historical data and synthetic simulator data is used.

6.1.4 Sensor Network Model

All the measuring nodes form an ad hoc network, and we need to select an appropriate network protocol that secures information exchange even in the presence of node failures. On top of the network protocol, a decision protocol is established. Both protocols are new parts of the system. The decision protocol is tested using generated and recorded earthquakes under the influence of applicable traffic noise.

In the node network model, simulation experiments are run with varying densities of nodes, failure rates, decision algorithms and network protocols. The model allows to check the handling of malfunction of sensors, the influence of sensor density and their associated cost and reliable communication between the sensors. In addition, we can confirm that the decision taken by the sensors is correct.

The network model uses random distributions for the delay and loss of the connections and the availability of nodes. The positions of nodes in the model correspond to locations on an actual map, with the assumption that the distances between the nodes represent their communication delays. As explained in Sect. 5.4, the same sensor node programs are used in the real environment, making them applicable and effective in the field.

6.1.5 Summary

Earthquakes are events causing serious damage. Like lightning comes before thunder, P-waves come before S-waves. This allows early warning for an earthquake as indicated in Fig. 6.1, which can protect critical infrastructure and prevent easily avoidable follow-up damage. Unfortunately, early warning technology is situated in the earthquake area and can be damaged. A decentralized ad hoc network of several self-organizing sensor nodes can survive major earthquakes. For this to work, we *program* the sensor nodes and test the embedded system in a virtual (*modelled*) environment. After this kind of test, the *system* works in reality the same as in the model, given that the model is correct in the perspective chosen.

6.2 Offshore Operations

In line with the general move towards digitization, also in offshore operations, the demand for autonomous and assisted operations is increasing. Modelling can help in this context. In this section, we look at the load handling in ship-to-ship operations in the open ocean as described in [29]. The problem solved is related to loading goods from one ship to another ship using a crane [27] (see Fig. 6.3). In this scenario, the positions of the ships are stabilized by some other means (GPS etc.). A similar operation is to move goods from a ship to an oil platform or vice versa. This seems simple enough, but we have to remember that this operation will be done in all weather conditions and with waves of considerable height. This means the operator of the crane has to take into account the movement of the goods and the movements of both ships due to the waves. The goal is to lift the goods smoothly and set them down equally smoothly. One of the two is simple, as the crane is attached to one of the ships. Working on the other ship is the difficult part of the exercise.

Fig. 6.3 Loading goods from one ship to another (©2024 Joachim Fischer inspired by https://www. youtube.com/watch?v=5_QoSTrU2gc – all rights reserved)

This kind of operation is not always possible – it is limited to be executed in a so-called weather window determining sensible limits. Currently, the limit is 2.5m significant wave height. Even within the weather window, loading the goods needs an experienced crane operator who knows how to adjust for the movements of the ships.

To improve operations, the crane operator is assisted by a tool [29], keeping the load at a fixed distance above the second ship deck while preventing the load from swinging such that the operator can concentrate on setting the goods down. This way, the assistant is part of an embedded system. With such compensation support, the weather window can be extended, and the safety and efficiency of the operations increase.

The compensation is based on the observation of the current state. The digital assistant needs information in real time: the movements of both ships (roll, heave, pitch), the load motions and the relative position and orientation of the ships.

The movements of the ships are captured using motion devices on both ships and a wireless transfer from the secondary ship to the primary ship. For the relative position of the ships, a laser tracker is employed. This is a device that can follow a moving target and determine the relative position of it. In our case, the tracker is placed on the primary ship and the target on the secondary ship. For better accuracy and redundancy, it is also possible to use several targets.

6.2.1 Perspective

Because our purpose is to move loads between ships, we only consider their loading area, which is essentially a plane in 3D. The primary ship has a crane mounted on the (loading area) plane. It has a movable boom and a jib, each with some length. There is a hook on a wire to attach the load. The waves are not part of the perspective. Instead, we only consider the movements of the ships, which means the movements of the two planes. The movement pattern depends on the average wave height.

6.2.2 Programming and Specification

There are two sources of control for the crane: the operator provides commands for the crane's movements towards the goal, while the assistant corrects for the relative motions of the two ships. This means that the assistant is programmed to adjust the crane and winch motion in such a way that the load is prevented from swinging and at the same time is kept in a controlled height above the receiving ship deck. This behaviour is similar to other assisting systems like adaptive cruise and steering control for cars.

The assistant observes the motions of the two ships and calculates their difference to estimate the load movements. This information is translated into crane controls (wire length, movement of the crane) that stabilize the operations, slightly adjusting the operator inputs.

The assistant correction is delayed to the original movement of the planes. Due to the slowness of the ship's movements, this does not pose problems. In addition, the current movement can be used to predict the position of the ship some time ahead, such that the crane movements can be smoother. Smooth crane movements are important to avoid swings. The assistant has to be designed carefully to avoid introducing swings because the operator cannot cancel swings that the assistant introduces.

The solution uses an Extended Kalman Filter [18] in the algorithm. The developed methods are described using a common and consistent mathematical notation for both the observers and the kinematic control systems.

6.2.3 Experiments

How can we validate that the assistant algorithm is correct? As this is difficult to do in real life, modelling comes to the rescue. There are three stages of testing: digital model, physical model and the final system as shown in Fig. 6.4 (see also Sect. 5.2). The first test is purely digital with models for waves, the ships, the crane and the load. The next test is hybrid with a real crane and load, and the ships are physically modelled (see below). Note how the ships are reduced to only one 3D plane as indicated by the perspective. After these tests, the product might also work in real waves, as long as the perspective is appropriate for the task. Still, we want to run tests there as well to confirm that everything works out well (see right side of Fig. 6.4).

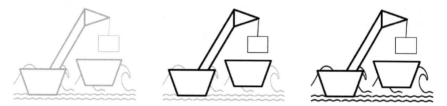

Fig. 6.4 Testing the ship-to-ship solution: digital-hybrid-real

6.2.4 Wave Model

For the digital and hybrid systems, we need a model of the environment, i.e. the waves and the movement of the ships on the waves. Such models are already available [14] and can be translated to a full six-degrees-of-freedom motion of the loading area plane of a ship (surge, sway, heave, roll, pitch and yaw). The simulated ship body motions result from random wave forces generated using the methods and techniques presented in [9].

Of course, for waves and even for the ship itself, it is also possible to get hold of real measurements over some time in diverse environmental conditions.

The simulated ship motions can be used in the digital system (Fig. 6.4 left). In the hybrid system (Fig. 6.4 middle), the ship motions are executed on physical Stewart platforms of the Norwegian Motion Laboratory [30][4] (see Fig. 6.5). These platforms have six degrees of freedom in 3D space and allow simulation of the three-dimensional movement of ships very well. We use one Stewart platform for the primary ship and one for the secondary ship. This setting allows to simulate ship movements on calm and stormy days by setting the significant wave height and wave period.

Fig. 6.5 Testing ship-to-ship operations using two Stewart platforms (©2024 Joachim Fischer inspired by https://www.motion-lab.no/ – all rights reserved)

6.2.5 Crane Program and Model

In the digital case (Fig. 6.4 left), a 3D model of the crane and its control is created to test different algorithms. The crane program is executed with this virtual crane, and its correctness can be checked in relevant scenarios. Please note that this involves the mathematical crane model (formulas) being described using code (programming).

6.2.6 Summary

Moving load from one ship to another in the open ocean is tricky due to the movements of the ships relative to each other based on the surrounding waves. A digital assistant is *programmed* to help the operator in this procedure by compensating the operator's commands for the movements of the ships, thereby also preventing the load

---

[4] https://www.motion-lab.no/

from swinging. Three increasing levels of reality are used in the *systems* constructed, starting with a purely digital system, continuing with a hybrid system and finishing with a purely physical system. This approach is often called 'model-based design' because physical *modelling* and simulation play major roles in the system development process. In this case, even the physical system has several digital elements, for example, the assistant.

6.3 Emergence of Bullying at a University

A bullying culture can exist in many contexts like school, family, the workplace, the home, neighbourhoods, on social media Web sites and even at universities [20, 24]. Bullying can involve physical, verbal, psychological (emotional) and cyber abuse, often leading to mental health problems and violence [36]. Therefore, many institutions want to avoid it, and some countries and states even have laws against it. However, existing intervention programs and proposed solutions so far have had mixed results [34].

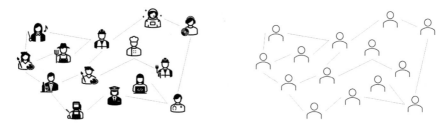

Fig. 6.6 An ABM replaces real people with virtual societies

Social phenomena like bullying are often difficult to study because social interactions emerge out of actions of individuals. Therefore, social scientists begin to use social models, in particular, agent-based models (ABM) [15] (see Fig. 6.6). Essentially, an ABM helps explore social theories by creating a 'virtual (modeled) society' by formalizing the tangible issues of the theory. Additionally, putting theories into a tool can integrate multiple disciplinary perspectives, which is crucial when dealing with complex interpersonal or inter-group conflicts.

In this section, we report on the use of the MARG ABM [39] to explore the emergence of bullying at a university in relation to the selection of interaction partners [38]. The purpose of the model was to understand the emergence of bullying and to identify meaningful interventions preventing this emergence (see also Sect. 3.2.3).

6.3.1 Mental Models

Currently, there are two dominant academic definitions of bullying. Olweus considers individual traits and defines bullying as the "negative actions" of one or multiple persons towards one person, "repeated" over time when the actor/s and the receptor of the behaviour have "asymmetric power relationship" [20]. Schott and Søndergaard think that bullying emerges from social dynamics and define it as "... an intensification of the processes of marginalisation that occur in the context of the dynamics of inclusion/exclusion, which shape groups. Bullying happens when physical, social, or symbolic exclusion becomes extreme, regardless of whether such exclusion is experienced and/or intended" [24] (see Fig. 6.7). In addition, perceptions of bullying differ between academics and non-academics [33].

Fig. 6.7 Bullying is understood as intense exclusion [24] (©2024 Joachim Fischer inspired by https://www.pinterest.com/pin/529735974892291814/ – all rights reserved)

Today, 'bullying' has evolved into an umbrella concept that accommodates various and quite diverse behaviours [38] like social exclusion, predatory sex crimes, mutual teasing and roughhousing. We want to understand if an innocent process such as interaction partner selection could lead to bullying, based on the second definition [24].

6.3.2 Perspective

An ABM organizes the subject matter knowledge around three main components: agents, attributes of environment and agents and behaviours including events. MARG ABM [39] models the concrete behaviour of marginalizing (excluding) students from interactions that take place in their free time within the space of the university, for example, during recess and group study. With this purpose, we reduce the relevant attributes.

Our agents are a number of students. Each student has a set of external (conspicuous) and internal (personal) characteristics. The external features are visible to all students, while the internal features can become known in interactions. A shared ideal set of external and internal values represents the cultural traits agents look for when interacting with others.

MARG considers positive, negative and refused interactions. Marginalization is the culmination of refused and negative interactions, counted as exclusion events. The interaction kind is based on the compatibility of the interaction partners. Students choose interaction partners based on the outcomes of previous interactions.

Each student has a tolerance window around the ideal values, which indicates the range of values acceptable for this student. Students are attracted to each other, which is kept with an attraction score. Students keep scores of their collected positive and negative interactions and remember the internal features of other students they have found. Initially, attraction is 50%, and all memories are empty.

Each time step represents a day (discrete time; see Sect. 4.3.1), and we observe the system for 100 days (one university semester). As bullying is intensified exclusion [24], we consider a student excluded with more than 80% negative or refused interactions. We look at group exclusion as the total percentage of excluded students.

6.3.3 Agent Model

There are two kinds of interactions between students: mandatory and voluntary. Students are paired randomly for interactions and have positive or negative results from them. In voluntary interactions, students choose whether they want to interact based on their attraction towards the other student. If the first student does not want to interact, the other student is unaware of the decision. Otherwise, if the other student refuses the interaction, the first will count this as a refused interaction.

A positive interaction increases the attraction, while a negative interaction decreases the attraction. The evaluation of the two students might differ. If a student finds the majority of characteristics of the other student within the tolerance window, then the interaction is positive; otherwise, it is negative. Learning more characteristics about the interaction partners will change the evaluations over time.

6.3.4 Experiments

An ABM called MARG was created with these rules and used to run several experiments [39]. Experiments were run with a realistic cultural norm (average traits match the norm) and an unrealistic one (norm outside the average). The unrealistic case has mostly negative interactions, leading to very high (almost 100%) average exclusion. Higher tolerance broadens the student's preferences and, thus, lowers exclusion. Higher diversity also lowers exclusion. A high tolerance combined with high diversity brings exclusion down to 83%.

The results are more diverse in the realistic scenario. Again, high tolerance reduces group exclusion because it broadens individual preferences. However, now, higher diversity leads to higher exclusion. Statistical analysis finds that only the diversity of agents' characteristics and tolerance have a significant effect on the percentage of excluded students. Both have antagonistic effects: as the diversity increases, the percentage of students excluded per simulation increases, and as the value of tolerance increases, the percentage of students excluded per simulation decreases.

6.3.5 Programming and Specification

The MARG ABM[5] was written in NetLogo[6], a language to describe and simulate agent-based models. Even though NetLogo is relatively simple for non-programmers to use, subject-matter experts, not skilled in computer programming, cannot read and validate the NetLogo code.

A better description for subject-matter experts is the Overview, Design concepts and Details (ODD) protocol as adopted in the ABM community [13]. ODD emerged as an effort to "make model descriptions more understandable and complete, thereby making ABMs less subject to criticism for being irreproducible". The protocol has seven thematic sections: "Purpose", "Entities, State Variables and Scales", "Process Overview and Scheduling", "Design Concepts", "Initialisation", "Input Data" and "Sub-models" [13]. Each section contains questions to guide modellers in the provision of related model details.

As an example, the section "Entity, State Variables, and Scales" poses the following questions: What kind of entities are in the model? Do they represent managers, voters, landowners, firms or something else? By what state variables or attributes are these entities characterized? What are the temporal and spatial resolutions and extents of the model?

The MARG model provides the following answers:

- The entities in this model are students.
- Students have a collection of external and internal characteristics.
- Each student has a tolerance and counters for positive, negative and refused interactions.
- Each model time unit denotes one day. The location of the students is irrelevant.

An ODD specification is informal but typically complete at the level of the perspective. The questions cover various aspects of the model to provide an understanding of what the model entails. The description in ODD is more readable for subject-matter experts and forms a domain-specific language (DSL) [10] for social simulation.

---

[5] https://github.com/themisdx/MARG

[6] http://ccl.northwestern.edu/netlogo/

The ODD2ABM tool [37] formalizes ODD. The text in the specification is roughly the same, but now it has semantics and can be executed. Technically, this is done using a compiler from ODD to NetLogo.

6.3.6 Summary

A formal *social model* will always create results. Therefore, it is important to make sure that the model is *correct* such that the model results match reality. The model is understandable for domain experts because it is written in a DSL which is *compiled* to an executable language.

We have shown that a model needs to be based on unambiguous *concepts*, actions and interactions. The formal model construction itself leads to reduced ambiguity. In the model, we used the concept of intensified marginalization instead of bullying, since bullying is more of a moral judgement than an action concept.

The MARG model presented here is quite simple and has serious limitations. Still, even this limited model showed the positive effect of tolerance on inclusion and the mixed effect of diversity on marginalization. Without putting marginalization into the model, it *emerged* as a result of the interactions.

6.4 Understanding and Managing Pandemic-Related Risks

In some cases, the complexity of a situation makes it challenging to determine the referent system. In such instances, constructing a model becomes intertwined with defining the referent system. This approach, known as strategy mapping, is discussed in detail in [4].

An example of such complexity arose during the COVID-19 pandemic when critical decisions needed to be made to address the situation. These decisions were based on assessing the direct and indirect risks posed to the health and social care systems due to the increasing number of COVID-19 cases and related mortality.

The situation was intricate because the risks and associated issues were interconnected, forming a complex network. In 2020, the SPRM (Systemic Pandemic Risk Management) research project, funded by the Research Council of Norway, delved into these interconnected issues and risks, exploring potential interventions. Further details about this project can be found in [1, 4, 23].

6.4.1 Perspective

When navigating the risks inherent in a pandemic, determining the most appropriate perspective is far from straightforward. With numerous risks at play, and mitigation efforts introducing additional variables, an interdisciplinary approach becomes imperative. This necessitates participatory modelling to shape the perspective of the referent system.

Initial interviews indicated the involvement of topics from over 70 disciplines in defining this perspective. Participants representing topics of several disciplines were selected to enable efficient group work. Ultimately, a group of 16 participants was assembled, covering all identified topics, with one member providing an 'outsider' viewpoint.

To establish a common perspective, causal dependencies between issues were identified. Participants articulated these issues, including various risks, using natural language. By focusing on issues and risks, it became easier to reconcile differing perspectives. Participants simultaneously contributed issues from their respective perspectives, resulting in a comprehensive system of issues encompassing all viewpoints, including several perspectives of the same participant.

Next, participants identified causal links between the issues, bridging different perspectives and facilitating the identification of expected outcomes and unforeseen consequences. In this step, participants gained a more holistic view of the referent system, simultaneously leveraging multiple perspectives and understanding others' viewpoints. After this first workshop established the perspective, the issues were grouped, and thematic clusters were selected.

6.4.2 Description

In this case, the worldview perspective (see Sect. 2.1) only includes causes and consequences between statements. This approach facilitates the incorporation of diverse purpose perspectives among participants, enabling a joint perspective.

The perspective is visualized as a causal map, with issues depicted as text boxes and causal dependencies represented by arrows linking the issues. To achieve this, the team utilized the tool Strategyfinder[7], which streamlined the collection and connection of participants' knowledge, effectively integrating their perspectives.

Strategyfinder can analyse causal maps, identify relevant feedback loops and group issues based on their interconnectedness. Furthermore, participants can employ various styles (font and colour) to categorize issues, such as identifying risks, goals, strategies, preferred options or key drivers of loops. Additionally, priorities can be assigned to issues, primarily focusing on risks in this context.

---

[7] https://www.strategyfinder.com/

6.4.3 Model

The second workshop started with the following subsystems (clusters) identified using Strategyfinder after the initial workshop:

- Low chance of international collaboration
- Shortage of healthcare workers (effectiveness per patient) in hospitals
- Low proportion of people (locally) getting properly vaccinated
- Increasing deterioration in mental health across the population
- Increased likelihood that criminals exploit the pandemic situation
- Breakdown of logistics (buses, rail, freight) – worse public service
- Lack of social cohesion
- Growing loss of public trust in authority (generally)
- Infodemics – overload on people, problems knowing what is true

In the model, all subsystems are connected to the two main outcomes to be avoided, namely:

- Increasing infection rates (the pandemic)
- Increasing indirect deaths from the pandemic

Each subsystem was examined individually, with participants adding missing information while validating and discussing existing issues and causal connections. This process allowed the initial workshops to concurrently establish both the perspective and the model of the situation. This collaborative effort resulted in a model for further detailed analysis of appropriate responses.

6.4.4 Programming

The final causal network (the model) is extensive, encompassing numerous issues, risks and their associated causes and outcomes. The network includes several feedback loops, which are of special importance because they can point to self-increasing (vicious cycles) or self-decreasing issues (virtuous cycles) (see also [12]).

While the initial two workshops aimed at comprehending the system, the subsequent two were dedicated to risk mitigation strategies. The objective was to devise (to program) strategies to address the identified risks effectively.

Strategyfinder was used to identify vicious cycles in the model, representing areas of heightened risk requiring special attention. It is crucial to address vicious cycles, as they signify a continual deterioration of the situation over time. Moreover, these cycles may interconnect, amplifying their impact and rendering them even more perilous.

Figure 6.8 shows a condensed representation of the 13 vicious cycles in the model. A sample vicious cycle starts with h, which causes k, which then causes l, which again causes h. This cycle is embedded in the bigger vicious cycle a, f, j, k, l, h, c, b, a, making it more dangerous. Strategyfinder detects issues b, d, f and j to be most

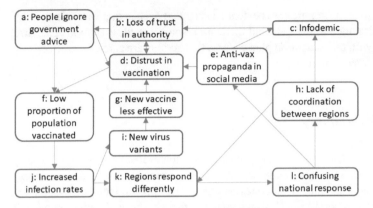

Fig. 6.8 Vicious cycles in the SPRM model (Adapted from [4, 26])

potent: mitigating all of them leaves only one vicious cycle, and mitigating any of them leaves only three vicious cycles.

Risk mitigation is done similarly to risk analysis: by adding new action issues. They also have causal connections with the existing issues and with each other. As before, an arrow represents a believed causal link between issues. To mitigate issue b, we consider the following three actions:

- Provide frequent information.
- Be open about the situation.
- Speak with one voice.

The complete network of risks and mitigation actions can now be analysed to check whether the actions will help reduce the risks and intercept the vicious cycles, maybe turning them into virtuous cycles.

As an example, when we introduce a "regular coordination activity between regions", the "coordination between regions" is strengthened, which leads to a "unified response from authorities" and then "less work locally with response plans", which again supports "regular coordination activity between regions". This turns the h-k-l vicious cycle into a virtuous cycle.

For mitigation, it is possible to introduce strategic issues that are realized with a portfolio of action issues having a causal link to that strategy.

When actions and strategies to mitigate the most prominent risks have been proposed, each participant evaluates the options by selecting a limited amount of preferred actions (simulating limited resources).

6.4.5 Using the Model

In the concluding workshop, the selected strategies from the previous session were reviewed, and participants were identified to take responsibility for their realization.

The model description was extended such that each action was linked to the specific risks it aimed to mitigate and the team responsible for execution. This direct alignment with the mitigation plan ensures that actions are carried out effectively to yield the desired outcomes.

6.4.6 Summary

Utilizing Strategyfinder, the project group achieved consensus on 25 strategies handling five key subsystems of risk, despite lacking prior collaborative experience. Notably, trust and social cohesion emerged as pivotal subsystems. A similar result was later reported in [3], which suggests that countries showing high levels of trust and social cohesion performed best under the challenges posed by the COVID-19 pandemic.

The project's success can be attributed to the seamless integration of *perspective* development with *model* construction. By collectively addressing issues and causal connections, participants forged a shared understanding of the risks at hand and identified the most effective mitigation strategies. Moreover, responsibilities for strategy realization were diligently assigned, facilitating the smooth *execution* of the (*programmed*) plan. The project's outcomes greatly satisfied the involved authorities, so they used the same approach in other contexts later.

6.5 Memorial Tour Modelling

Museums are public places designed to educate and entertain visitors through exhibits. Visitor flow is regulated using specific structures like registration counters, waiting areas and a gift shop close to the exit. Visitors interact with these structures, starting with registration and ticket purchase, exploring exhibits and ending at the gift shop.

Guided tours are also offered, where a guide leads visitors through exhibits, providing explanations and background information. With some freedom for the guide, the route and the exhibits to visit are given in a tour plan, because the exhibits and rooms are shared resources and can often only be visited by one group at a time. Limitations can go beyond individual exhibits, for example, narrow passages that can only be used by one group at a time or adjacent exhibits that do not allow simultaneous visits by two groups. Tour plans for guides ensure that disturbances are minimized.

The Berlin-Hohenschönhausen Memorial[8] serves not only as a museum but also as a reminder of the political oppression endured in East Germany, as it was the primary political prison of that era. In this section, we focus on its role as a museum.

---

[8] https://www.stiftung-hsh.de/en/

The memorial is a complex of buildings housing numerous small rooms, each serving as a prison cell, connected by long corridors (see Fig. 6.9). Due to its location within a historical building, the memorial is not designed to accommodate large crowds of visitors. Consequently, the museum exclusively offers guided tours to manage visitor flow efficiently. While this limitation restricts visitors from freely exploring the premises, it allows the museum to organize guided tours in groups. The available tour options enable visitors to choose based on their schedule and interests.

Fig. 6.9 Corridor in the Berlin-Hohenschönhausen Memorial and cell door (©2024 Joachim Fischer inspired by [19] – all rights reserved)

The museum employs specific guidelines to schedule tours and allocate guides, some of whom are witnesses with firsthand experience as former prisoners in the memorial. By offering different start times for groups, the museum effectively manages visitor flow. However, receptionists often face the challenging task of determining the feasibility of a tour by assessing whether potential delays in visitor movements remain within acceptable limits.

Given the substantial volume of tours conducted daily (exceeding 2000 visitors), coordinating them manually is impractical and necessitates computer assistance. To address this challenge, a model of the museum has been developed, enabling simulation of group tours and subsequent evaluation of potential delays. Further details on this project can be found in [19].

6.5.1 Perspective

We focus on *tour plans*, which are a subset of the complete *tour graph* of the museum, consisting of the available *stations* and their connections (*passages*) (see Fig. 6.10). The museum has *guides* and *witnesses*, but for our purpose, only their capacity is relevant. Similarly, for the visitors, only their speed and group size are essential.

Stations can be *exhibits*, *waiting areas*, ticket *desks* and *seminar rooms*. Passages
that can be blocked by a group are handled as special stations called *switch*.

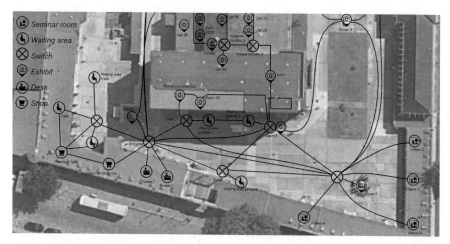

Fig. 6.10 Partial impression of the tour graph of the Berlin-Hohenschönhausen Memorial (©2024
Moritz Lemm overlay over a Satellite image of the Memorial – all rights reserved)

We ignore all other aspects of the memorial, for example, the weather, rooms that
are not open or not used, the age of the guides and the gender of the visitors.

6.5.2 Static Model

We collect all elements of the perspective in a SysML diagram, as shown in Fig. 6.11.
In addition, we also consider the following elements:

- Stations have capacities for visitors and the average duration of stay (delay).
  Exhibits indicate their capacity as the number of permissible groups, while waiting
  areas and seminar rooms use the number of persons. The delay is a random
  distribution (see also Sect. 4.3.5).
- Tour plans can contain branches for dynamic choices depending on the load of
  the stations. They do not appear in Fig. 6.11, because they are just restricted tour
  graphs.
- A guide cannot handle groups bigger than 25 people. The limit comes from the
  ability to talk to that many people in the open outside areas and the limited size
  of the prison cells.
- A *booking* is a binding contract for a planned visit to the museum. It includes the
  timing information required for planning and via the guided tour the group size,
  guide and tour plan.
- The *timetable* is the set of all registered bookings.

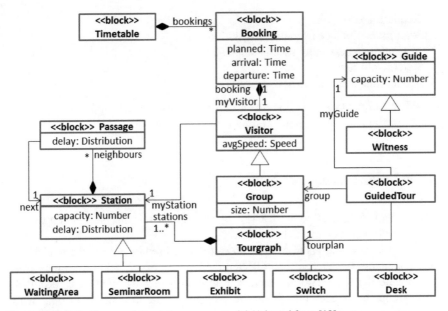

Fig. 6.11 SysML diagram of the static museum model (Adapted from [19]

- A *guided tour* connects a group with a guide and a tour plan. Via the group, it also has a booking.
- Visitors store *myStation* as an RTS element (see Sect. 5.1.2).

The distributions of the delays at the stations and between the stations and the capacity of stations have been determined using observations of the actual guided tours in a field study over a week. In addition, interviews have been performed with guides for the same information.

6.5.3 Dynamic Model

A visit to the memorial starts with visitors gathering at the registration area where they are assigned to a tour group, predetermined by their booking. Individual visitors without a booking must join one of the public guided tours.

Following registration, visitors await their tour's commencement by viewing a 30-minute video presentation in the seminar room. Subsequently, the group meets their guide who leads them on the planned museum tour, lasting approximately 90 minutes. Finally, visitors wait again, browsing the museum shop or exploring the exhibition area, before exiting the museum.

From our perspective, groups navigate through the museum, with guides serving as a resource accompanying them throughout the experience. In the model, a group travels the guided tour repeating the following steps:

1. Request next station.
2. Wait for acceptance from the next station.
3. Transition to next station with some delay.
4. Release old station.
5. Model time delay at the new station (optional).

When waiting takes too long, the group can choose another option from the tour plan, for example, select another possible prison cell to visit.

6.5.4 Programming and Experiments

The model is programmed in SLX [17] by a computer scientist, such that it was not problematic that code had to be written.

First, the observations from the field study were used to validate the model until the model results matched the collected data. Then, experiments were performed to evaluate the load. Two parameters were considered: the number of deadlocks (two groups block each other) and the average waiting time in the model. Below five groups per hour, the load was not noticeable, and above ten, the waiting time increased exponentially. The model can be used in the booking process to find out whether a new booking will lead to problems.

6.5.5 Summary

This section presented a *model* to analyse guided tours within a museum setting based on a dedicated museum simulator framework. Through various *experiments*, the framework was employed to assess the feasibility of existing and new (*programmed*) tour plans and *predict* their performance under peak visitation periods.

The model represents the architectural layout of the museum, dynamically accommodating tour plans and integrating real or simulated booking schedules. Delays and arrival times are simulated as *random distributions*, informed by empirical data.

The metric used to gauge visitor load includes delays and deadlocks, even though deadlocks are solved in practice in some way. The results help the booking system manage visitor flow effectively, minimizing tensions between guides and visitors and ensuring a smooth tour experience.

6.6 Notre-Dame

Notre-Dame is a medieval Catholic cathedral on the Île de la Cité in Paris. Its full name Notre-Dame de Paris translates to 'Our Lady of Paris'. This remarkable Gothic structure is dedicated to the Virgin Mary and has magnificent features such as its vast, colourful rose windows, intricate sculptural decorations, three pipe organs and colossal church bells. Being an iconic symbol of Paris and France, Notre-Dame attracts approximately 12 million visitors annually. Victor Hugo's renowned novel *The Hunchback of Notre-Dame* is famously set within its walls.

Tragically, in 2019, a devastating fire broke out during renovations. After 15 hours of fire, the cathedral had sustained serious damage (see Fig. 6.12). The French government pledged to rebuild the cathedral to its original state, igniting a global effort to reclaim this historic landmark. However, restoring such a treasured monument is challenging. While historical documents and sketches offer insights into the cathedral's construction process, and numerous photographs document its various elements, these resources provide only fragmented glimpses of Notre-Dame's grandeur. Can a model of the cathedral be used for the restoration?

Fig. 6.12 Notre-Dame before and after the fire (©2024 Joachim Fischer – all rights reserved)

The computer game *Assassin's Creed Unity* [31] offers detailed 3D models of numerous historical landmarks in Paris, including Notre-Dame Cathedral. The game is set in Paris during the French Revolution, providing players with a virtual tour of the cathedral and allowing them to explore its intricate details. Leveraging these detailed models could be a remarkable foundation for the restoration efforts [16].

6.6.1 Perspective

For the restoration purpose, adopting a builder's perspective is essential. This entails careful consideration of the materials utilized, the specific components chosen and their external appearance. Moreover, the assembly process of these components is significant within this context.

We assume that achieving the desired final appearance and structural integrity is prioritized over adhering strictly to medieval construction techniques. Therefore, selecting materials that closely resemble the originals is crucial, as emphasized in [22]. This extends to the materials employed for bonding the building blocks together.

Given the enduring nature of medieval structures, modern materials must be selected carefully.

6.6.2 Game 3D Model

The 3D model of Notre-Dame featured in the game serves a distinct purpose from reconstructing the actual building, thereby achieving a different perspective. Its purpose is to evoke the look and feel of the historic structure while navigating it for various gameplay tasks.

As described in [16], Ubisoft's designers, artists and historians dedicated years to meticulously recreating the Notre-Dame Cathedral in the game. This virtual rendition allows tourists to explore the cathedral virtually, offering an immersive experience before or instead of physical travel to Paris. The in-game model is complete from the perspective of the game including intricate details such as statues, pew layouts and stained glass windows [16].

6.6.3 Historical Correctness

The game's Notre-Dame model is not entirely accurate [32]. The gameplay focus emphasized capturing the essence of the building rather than every precise detail. For instance, the spire's design is not historically correct, resembling the modern version rather than its smaller, wooden predecessor. This particular inconsistency is an advantage for the current task to recreate the destroyed spire in its modern form.

Furthermore, accommodations were made in the game to facilitate player movement, such as additional cables and incense across the second level for easier traversal [32]. Additionally, interactive elements like opening stained-glass windows and guiding gilt panels were incorporated to aid player navigation [5]. The intricate sculptures above the cathedral's main doors pose a challenge for real-time rendering. The game shows them as flat structures with intricate textures, giving the illusion of depth until viewed up close [5].

Due to France's copyright laws, many aspects of the game's artwork *must not* precisely mirror the original Notre-Dame. This applies to elements like the organ and the rose windows [5, 32], leading designers to reinterpret these features to offer a similar experience within legal constraints. Caroline Miousse, senior level artist on *Assassin's Creed Unity*, states in [32]: 'It gave me the opportunity to create something new from a starting point that people know and understand. It was a very interesting challenge and I had a lot of fun with it'. Maxime Durand, Ubisoft's resident art historian, emphasized in an interview with Le Monde that 'The monument that we recreated takes great artistic liberty' [2].

Despite these deviations from historical accuracy, the game's Notre-Dame model nicely resembles the original, fulfilling its intended purpose to be a compelling and immersive representation of the iconic cathedral. However, the game model seems to fail the purpose of helping real-life researchers restore the damaged cathedral.

6.6.4 Description

The game model is crafted and programmed within the Ubisoft Anvil game engine[9]. Within Anvil, the environment is modelled using 3ds Max[10], while character modelling is accomplished in ZBrush[11], coupled with Autodesk's HumanIK[12] middleware for positioning characters' hands and feet during animations. This setup underscores the dynamic nature of the game model, which responds to player actions and environmental variables such as weather and time of day.

Anvil received an upgrade in 2012, known as AnvilNext, introducing numerous new features, including the automatic rendering of landmarks like Notre-Dame. However, the Notre-Dame de Paris representation is still crafted by hand.

The requirements for restoration differ considerably. As Cédric Gachaud explained to Le Monde [2], '... we're looking for millimeter precision'. His company, Life3D, had been developing 3D models of Notre-Dame before the fire. Notable models also exist within academia, including one by art historian Andrew Tallon, based on laser scans, high-resolution images and other data sources [21]. These datasets, combined with new scans and photographs, are integral to the reconstruction process.

However, raw data alone does not constitute a model. By inputting the data into a 3D engine, a navigable model is generated, adaptable for various purposes, including visualizing the envisioned outcome of the restoration. Yet, for the actual reconstruction of Notre-Dame, skilled craftsmen such as woodworkers, stonemasons and artisans are indispensable. This necessitates another kind of dynamism in the model. While data collection primarily aims to capture a static snapshot of the structure, the reconstruction process is dynamic, demanding additional efforts beyond mere snapshot descriptions.

6.6.5 Summary

We've explored three interconnected systems: the original Notre-Dame before the fire, the forthcoming restored version and the virtual game rendition.

Initially, the game version served as a *model* of the original structure, offering a compelling and immersive experience for tourists worldwide. While historical *cor-*

---

9 https://en.wikipedia.org/wiki/Ubisoft_Anvil

10 https://en.wikipedia.org/wiki/Autodesk_3ds_Max

11 https://en.wikipedia.org/wiki/ZBrush

12 https://en.wikipedia.org/wiki/Autodesk_Gameware

rectness wasn't paramount for its intended use, the game model effectively conveyed the essence of Notre-Dame, sparking curiosity and prompting further exploration. Despite inaccuracies in details like sculptures and rose windows, these deviations were inconsequential in eliciting the emotional resonance of Notre-Dame.

However, emotional authenticity doesn't equate to historical fidelity. For the restoration project, historical accuracy is paramount, demanding meticulous attention to materials, construction techniques and architectural correctness. This necessitates collaboration among scientists, scholars and experts to establish the *perspective* for the restoration including the needed precision.

Lastly, from a gaming perspective, Notre-Dame is an ideal setting for immersive gameplay, offering ample nooks and crannies for adventurous exploits. The game developers crafted a virtual cathedral, drawing from real-world blueprints to create an authentic gaming experience.

Acknowledgements We extend our gratitude to Dorian Weber for his support in crafting Sects. 6.1 and 6.5. Additionally, we appreciate the contributions of Sondre Sanden Tørdal to Sect. 6.2 and the assistance provided by Themis Xanthopoulou in shaping Sect. 6.3. Furthermore, we acknowledge the contributions of Jose Gonzalez to the development of Sect. 6.4, Moritz Lemm to Sect. 6.5 and Tobias Michael Scholz to Sect. 6.6.

Exercises

6.1 (Flight Simulator) A flight simulator is software that allows one to experience flying a plane. Simple versions work like games, while advanced versions use real cockpits to recreate the flight feeling as exactly as possible. After extended training in a flight simulator, a real flight is manageable[13].
Discuss flight simulators in terms of the concepts of this book. What is the associated perspective, what is the modelling involved and where are the programming and descriptions?

6.2 (Maps) Assume you use a map to plan a hiking trip.
Discuss your plan and the map as a model of the trip in terms of the concepts of this book. What is the associated perspective, what is the modelling involved and where are the programming and descriptions?

6.3 (Human Models) When you search the Internet for the term 'models', your first hits will relate to the profession or role to be a model.
Discuss these human models in terms of the concepts of this book. What is the associated perspective, what is the modelling involved and where are the programming and descriptions?

6.4 (Weather Forecast) Consider your favourite weather forecast site. It provides a description of the weather to come and maybe also of the weather that has been.

---

[13] The following experience report explains how the flight simulator experience differs from the real flight: https://qr.ae/pysgSx.

Discuss weather forecasts in terms of the concepts of this book. What is the associated perspective, what is the modelling involved and where are the programming and descriptions?

References

1. Abildsnes, E., Paulsen, S., Gonzalez, J.J.: Improving resilience against a pandemic: a novel technology for strategy development with practitioners and decision-makers. In: Proceedings of the International ISCRAM Conference 2023, pp. 964–974 (2023)
2. Audureau, W.: No, the video game *Assassin's Creed Unity* does not help reconstruct Notre-Dame de Paris (in French). Le Monde (2019)
3. Bollyky, T.J., Ma, L.Y., Sweat, S., Bradshaw, M.J., Moss, W.J., Omer, S.B., Wesolowski, A., Eagle, N., Lipsitch, M.: Pandemic preparedness and covid-19: an exploratory analysis of infection and fatality rates, and contextual factors associated with preparedness in 177 countries, from Jan 1, 2020, to Sept 30, 2021. Lancet **399**(10334), 1489–1512 (2022). https://doi.org/10.1016/S0140-6736(22)00172-6
4. Bryson, J.M.: Addressing Complex and Cross-Boundary Challenges in Government: The Value of Strategy Mapping. IBM Center for the Business of Government (2023)
5. de Rochefort, S.: *Assassin's Creed Unity* can't help rebuild Notre-Dame, and that's ok (2021). https://www.polygon.com/features/22790314. Accessed 30 May 2024
6. Erdik, M., Fahjan, Y., Ozel, O., Alcik, H., Mert, A., Gul, M.: Istanbul earthquake rapid response and the early warning system. Bull. Earthquake Eng. **1**, 157–163 (2003). https://doi.org/10.1023/A:1024813612271
7. Fischer, J., Kühnlenz, F., Ahrens, K., Eveslage, I.: Model-based development of self-organizing earthquake early warning systems. Simul. Notes Eur. **19**(3–4), 9–20 (2009). https://doi.org/10.11128/sne.19.on.09941
8. Fischer, J., Redlich, J.P., Zschau, J., Milkereit, C., Picozzi, M., Fleming, K., Brumbulli, M., Lichtblau, B., Eveslage, I.: A wireless mesh sensing network for early warning. J. Netw. Comput. Appl. **35**(2), 538–547 (2012). https://doi.org/10.1016/j.jnca.2011.07.016. Simulation and Testbeds
9. Fossen, T.: Handbook of Marine Craft Hydrodynamics and Motion Control. Wiley, London (2021)
10. Fowler, M.: Domain-Specific Languages. Addison-Wesley Professional, Reading (2010)
11. Gasparini, P., Manfredi, G., Zschau, J.: Earthquake Early Warning Systems. Springer, Berlin (2007)
12. Gonzalez, J.J., Eden, C.: Insights from the covid-19 pandemic for systemic risk assessment and management. In: Sasaki, J., Murayama, Y., Velev, D., Zlateva, P. (eds.) Information Technology in Disaster Risk Reduction, pp. 121–138. Springer, Cham (2022)
13. Grimm, V., Berger, U., DeAngelis, D.L., Polhill, J.G., Giske, J., Railsback, S.F.: The ODD protocol: A review and first update. Ecol. Model. **221**(23), 2760–2768 (2010). https://doi.org/10.1016/j.ecolmodel.2010.08.019
14. Guo, Q., Xu, Z.: Simulation of deep-water waves based on JONSWAP spectrum and realization by MATLAB. In: 2011 19th International Conference on Geoinformatics, pp. 1–4 (2011). https://doi.org/10.1109/GeoInformatics.2011.5981100
15. Hamill, L.: Agent-based modelling: the next 15 years. J. Artif. Soc. Soc. Simul. **13**(4), 11 (2010). https://doi.org/10.18564/jasss.1640
16. Handy, K.: Bridging the gap between gaming and history: How assassin's creed unity is helping rebuild Notre-Dame. https://www.artstation.com/blogs/dioeye/1dYG (2023). Accessed 30 May 2024
17. Henriksen, J.O.: SLX: the x is for extensibility [simulation software]. In: Simulation Conference, 2000. Proceedings. Winter, vol. 1, pp. 183–190 vol.1 (2000). https://doi.org/10.1109/WSC.2000.899715

18. Kim, P.: Kalman Filter for Beginners: With MATLAB Examples. CreateSpace Independent Publishing Platform (2007)
19. Lemm, M.W.: Modelling and simulation of museum tours (in German). Master's Thesis, Humboldt-University of Berlin (2019). https://sar.informatik.hu-berlin.de/research/publications/#SAR-PR-2019-01
20. Olweus, D.: Aggressive Behavior: Current Perspectives, pp. 97–130. Springer, Boston (1994). https://doi.org/10.1007/978-1-4757--9116-7_5
21. Pollock, E.: Inside the model that may help restore Notre-Dame (2023). https://www.engineering.com/story/inside-the-model-that-may-help-restore-notre-dame. Accessed 30 May 2024
22. Rea, N.: Can 'Assassin's Creed' help rebuild Notre-Dame? How restoring the cathedral will rely on both new tech and ancient knowhow (2019). https://news.artnet.com/market/how-technologies-old-and-new-will-be-needed-to-rebuild-notre-dame-1520689. Accessed 30 May 2024
23. Research Council of Norway: SPRM - systemic pandemic risk management. https://prosjektbanken.forskningsradet.no/en/project/FORISS/315444. Accessed 30 May 2024
24. Schott, R.M., Søndergaard, D.M. (eds.): School Bullying: New Theories in Context. Cambridge University Press, Cambridge (2014). https://doi.org/10.1017/CBO9781139226707
25. Shearer, P.M.: Introduction to Seismology, 3rd edn. Cambridge University Press, Cambridge (2019). https://doi.org/10.1017/9781316877111
26. Strategyfinder: Systemic risk management with Strategyfinder. https://www.strategyfinder.com/why-you-need-strategyfinder/systemic-risk-management/. Accessed 30 May 2024
27. The Port of Scandinavia: Ship to ship transfers - Port of Gothenburg. https://www.goteborgshamn.se/FileDownload/?contentReferenceID=13816
28. The SeisSol Team: Seissol. https://seissol.readthedocs.io/en/latest/index.html
29. Tørdal, S.S.: Real-time motion compensation in ship-to-ship load handling. Ph.D. Thesis, University of Agder (2019). https://uia.brage.unit.no/uia-xmlui/handle/11250/2590151
30. Tørdal, S.S., Olsen, J.T., Hovland, G.: The Norwegian motion-laboratory. Model. Identif. Control **39**(1), 21–29 (2018). https://doi.org/10.4173/mic.2018.1.3
31. Ubisoft Montreal: *Assassin's Creed Unity* (2014)
32. Ubisoft News: How Ubisoft re-created Notre-Dame for 'Assassin's Creed Unity' (2019). https://blog.siggraph.org/2019/05/how-ubisoft-re-created-notre-dame-for-assassins-creed-unity.html/. Accessed 30 May 2024
33. Vaillancourt, T., McDougall, P., Hymel, S., Krygsman, A., Miller, J., Stiver, K., Davis, C.: Bullying: are researchers and children/youth talking about the same thing? Int. J. Behav. Devel. **32**(6), 486–495 (2008). https://doi.org/10.1177/0165025408095553
34. Vreeman, R.C., Carroll, A.E.: A systematic review of school-based interventions to prevent bullying. Arch. Pediatr. Adolesc. Med. **161**(1), 78–88 (2007). https://doi.org/10.1001/archpedi.161.1.78
35. Wang, R.: A simple orthonormalization method for stable and efficient computation of green's functions. Bull. Seismol. Soc. Am. **89**(3), 733–741 (1999)
36. Wolke, D., Lereya, S.T.: Long-term effects of bullying. Arch. Disease Childhood **100**(9), 879–885 (2015)
37. Xanthopoulou, T.D., Prinz, A., Shults, F.L.: Generating executable code from high-level social or socio-ecological model descriptions. In: Fonseca i Casas, P., Sancho, M.R., Sherratt, E. (eds.) System Analysis and Modeling. Languages, Methods, and Tools for Industry 4.0, vol. 11753, pp. 150–162. Springer, Cham (2019). https://doi.org/10.1007/978-3-030-30690-8_9
38. Xanthopoulou, T.D., Prinz, A., Shults, F.L.: The problem with bullying: lessons learned from modelling marginalization with diverse stakeholders. In: Czupryna, M., Kamiński, B. (eds.) Advances in Social Simulation, pp. 289–300. Springer, Berlin (2022)
39. Xanthopoulou, T.D., Puga-Gonzalez, I., Shults, F.L., Prinz, A.: Modeling marginalization: emergence, social physics, and social ethics of bullying. In: 2020 Spring Simulation Conference (SpringSim), pp. 1–12. IEEE, Piscataway (2020). https://doi.org/10.22360/SpringSim.2020.HSAA.005

Chapter 7
Summary

> Writing long books is a laborious and impoverishing act of foolishness: expanding in five hundred pages an idea that could be perfectly explained in a few minutes. A better procedure is to pretend that those books already exist and to offer a summary, a commentary.
>
> Jorge Luis Borges

Models and specifications are everywhere. We reduce the complexity of reality to what we can grasp, using concepts, abstractions and analogies [6]. This book is no different; it also invites you to follow a model – this time, a model of modelling and programming. There are other ways to approach modelling, and different disciplines have different ideas about this [1, 2, 4, 5, 7, 9, 13–18, 20].

Using models in science, we can understand reality, and by using models in engineering, we can create reality. It might seem that these two uses of models are different, but they are very similar and based on three essential relationships as shown in Fig. 7.1.

1. First, it is important to acknowledge that there is a divide between reality and our perception of it, using our own or extending the senses. This leads us to consider *perspective* as a filter (the glasses) composed of worldview and purpose [19]. Applying perspective to reality ends up with a system (Chap. 2). Systems can be of different kinds, for example, physical, digital or mental.
2. Second, systems can be compared based on a perspective, and when they match, we call them models [16]. A *model* is a system that matches another system, called referent system (Chap. 3). Mental models are an important category of models [8]. These models exist in our minds and provide a match with reality depending on our perspective.
3. Third, systems can be created using *descriptions* (Chap. 4). There is a wide variety of descriptions, with many disciplines having developed their own languages for

A. Prinz et al., *Understanding Modelling and Programming*,
https://doi.org/10.1007/978-3-031-71280-7_7

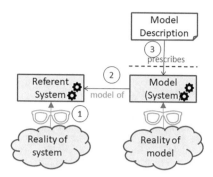

Fig. 7.1 Three relationships covered in the book

descriptions of their systems, commonly called domain-specific language [9]. A description means something; it *prescribes* a system via its semantics. The semantics of a description belongs to its language. Descriptions can be on different levels of formality, such that the description more or less precisely defines the resulting system.

The process of creating a description (or specification) of a system is called *programming* (Chap. 5, [10]). The idea of programming is to create a system; the description is the means to this end. In Fig. 7.1, programming is a vertical connection. This way, programming reverses the semantics connection, creating a description for an intended system. The prescribed system is a model of the intended (referent) system. In a narrow sense, programming means creating computer code prescribing a digital system by executing the code.

Modelling [4] means creating a model of a referent system and is a horizontal connection in Fig. 7.1. In engineering, modelling is most often understood as creating a description of a model of a referent system. Even with this understanding, the intended result is not the description but the prescribed system (the model).

Now we want to look at some *pitfalls* related to modelling and programming. Many of those problems have been identified earlier (see [12, 18] and the figures in [11]).

- Mistaking our perspective for reality: We want to stress that *systems are not the reality* (Sect. 2.1, [19]). They are a perspective on some part of reality. A perspective cannot be correct, but it can be useful. When there are different perspectives on the same reality, all of them can be useful, but none of them captures reality fully. For example, we can watch a car as a means of transport, a piece of art or a culprit for global warming.
- Thinking that our perspective is the truth: Since we handle reality via systems, we can easily *change reality by changing our perspective* (Sect. 2.1). This can often help us understand reality better, find solutions to problems or solve conflicts. Lateral thinking [3] is one way to change perspective. For example, changing perspective from geocentric to heliocentric allowed a better explanation of the movements of the celestial bodies.

- Using a model outside its scope: A model uses some perspective and relates to a referent system within this perspective. We can extend the perspective for the model, but that does not mean the model-of relationship extends. Therefore, *extending a model beyond its original perspective might invalidate correctness* (Sect. 3.2, [18]). For example, cooking time is a good indicator of the softness of an egg when cooking at sea level. However, extending the model to high altitudes does not match reality, as the boiling temperature is lower such that the needed cooking time is longer.
- Believing in far-fetched model consequences: *Results in a model might not apply to reality* because they represent the perspective used for creating the model (Sect. 3.2.3). For example, it was believed for a long time that the sound barrier could not be broken by airplanes [11].
- Confusing the model with reality: The relation between a model and its referent system is symmetric (Sects. 3.1 and 5.1), which might invite us to *mistake the model for reality*, leading to confusion [12]. This is a typical mistake made by clerks. For example, if we define age as the number of birthdays a person had, then a 24-year-old born on February 29 could be invited to school because the age in the model is 6.
- Falling in love with one model: When we want to handle the complexity of reality, a single model is deficient. *Using more than one model helps understand reality better*, even if the models are conflicting (Sects. 3.1 and 6.4, [2, 7, 18]). For example, the nature of light can be described as a wave or a particle stream. Both models contradict each other, but jointly they provide a good understanding of the nature of light.
- Confusing a description with reality: *A model description is not reality* (Sect. 2.3). The description prescribes a model, which relates to reality. The description cannot be used instead of the reality. For example, one does not strike oil by drilling through the map [12].
- Mistaking the limits of language for limits of reality: Using a specific language for your description restricts what can be expressed [9]. *If you cannot express a system in your language, it does not mean it does not exist* (Sects. 2.3, 3.1 and 5.1). For example, square roots of negative numbers cannot be expressed in real numbers but are fine in complex numbers.

This book has discussed modelling and programming from several points of view.

- From a *systems* point of view, a system is an interactive collection of parts, which can be existing or new. The parts and their connection are given by the perspective applied. By definition, this is also true for models. A system must include all relevant parts of reality for the purpose. Computer science often avoids looking at system parts outside the computer, but these must be included in the (embedded) systems we consider. System analysis, testing and validation depend on a comprehensive perspective [5, 14].
- From a *description* and *language* point of view, systems can be created using a specification [17]. The specification *prescribes* the system based on the semantics of the description. All *descriptions* are written using one or more languages. These

languages provide semantics connecting each description with its prescribed system.

• From a *correctness* point of view, a model must match the referent system [1]. When the referent system of a model is based on a description itself, it is possible to compare the model and the referent system by analysing their descriptions. This process, called verification, lifts the model-of relationship onto the syntactic level. When the referent system is not based on a description, formal proof is impossible, and validation, also called testing, is the only choice for establishing the correctness of the model-of relationship.

This book provides the concepts and tools for complete and correct modelling and programming. However, the proof of the pudding is in the eating, and the understanding must be applied in practical cases.

References

1. Bellomo, N., Tezduyar, T.E. (eds.): Modeling and Simulation in Science, Engineering and Technology. Book Series. Springer, Berlin (2006–2024). https://www.springer.com/series/4960
2. Close, C.M.: Modeling and Analysis of Dynamic Systems. Wiley, London (2010)
3. de Bono, E.: Lateral Thinking: Creativity Step by Step. Harper Perennial (1970)
4. Embley, D., Thalheim, B.: Handbook of Conceptual Modeling: Theory, Practice, and Research Challenges. Springer, Berlin (2012)
5. Gianni, D., D'Ambrogio, A., Tolk, A. (eds.): Modeling and Simulation-Based Systems Engineering Handbook. CRC Press, Boca Raton (2014)
6. Hofstadter, D.R.: Surfaces and Essences: Analogy as the Fuel and Fire of Thinking. Basic Books, New York (2013)
7. Hybertson, D.W.: Model-Oriented Systems Engineering Science: A Unifying Framework for Traditional and Complex Systems. Taylor and Francis, New York (2009)
8. Johnson-Laird, P.: Mental models: Toward a Cognitive Science of Language, Inference and Consciousness. Cambridge University Press, Cambridge (1983)
9. Kelly, S., Tolvanen, J.: Domain-Specific Modeling—Enabling Full Code Generation. Wiley, London (2008)
10. Knuth, D.: The Art of Programming I–VI. Addison-Wesley, Reading (1968-2015)
11. Kristiansson, L.: Linear Models for Analogue and Digital Systems (in Swedish). Chalmers University, Department of Information Theory, Gothenburg (1977)
12. Lee, E.A.: Plato and the Nerd: The Creative Partnership of Humans and Technology. MIT Press, Cambridge (2017)
13. Rothenberg, J.: The Nature of Modeling. A Rand note. The RAND Corporation (1989). https://books.google.no/books?id=wc7qAAAAMAAJ
14. Samuel, A., Weir, J.: Introduction to Engineering Design: Modelling, Synthesis and Problem Solving Strategies. Elsevier, Amsterdam (2000)
15. Sokolowski, J.A., Banks, C.M.: Modeling and Simulation for Analyzing Global Events. Wiley, London (2009)
16. Stachowiak, R.: General Model Theory. Springer, Berlin (1973)
17. Stahl, T., Völter, M.: Model-Driven Software Development: Technology, Engineering, Management. Wiley, Chichester (2006)
18. Thompson, E.: Escape from Model Land: How Mathematical Models Can Lead Us Astray and What We Can Do About It. Basic Books (2022)
19. Watzlawick, P., Birkenbihl, V.F.: How Real Is Real? Confusion, Disinformation, Communication. Random House (1976)
20. Wellstead, P.E.: Introduction to Physical System Modelling. Academic Press, London (1979)

Glossary

Compiler Definition 5.4 on page 63: A *compiler* is a specification (a program) describing how to translate a specification in a language L to a semantically equivalent specification in another language ML.

Correctness Definition 3.4 on page 26: Model *correctness* is the similarity of the model executions with the referent system executions based on the model-of relationship and the perspective.

Description Definition 2.5 on page 14: A *description* is a statement or account about the characteristics of an object or system.

Execution Definition 2.4 on page 11: An *execution* of a system is an observation of a system over a period of time with a given time granularity. This way, an execution is a collection of system snapshots at the time points of the time granularity.

Experiment Definition 3.5 on page 27: An *experiment* is a set of conditions for a system execution, specifying the starting state, end conditions, and values for system attributes.

Interpreter Definition 5.3 on page 62: An *interpreter* is a specification (a program) describing how to read and execute a specification in a language L.

Language Definition 4.1 on page 35: A *language* is a set of descriptions together with their semantics.

Machine Definition 5.2 on page 61: A *machine* is an entity that executes a specification.

Meaning Definition 3.8 on page 30: The *meaning* of a model element description is the referent element to which the prescribed model refers. It depends on both the prescribed system and the referent system and is hence not unique.

Model Definition 3.2 on page 22: A *model* is a system that is in the *model-of* relationship to a referent system, existing or planned, where the model-of relationship means that the model is *analogous* to and *more focused* than the referent system.

© The Author(s), under exclusive license to Springer Nature Switzerland AG 2025
A. Prinz et al., *Understanding Modelling and Programming*,
https://doi.org/10.1007/978-3-031-71280-7

Two systems are analogous when they have similar behaviour in their similar perspectives, and a system is more focused than another (analogous) system if it uses fewer objects, fewer attributes, or both.

Modelling Definition 3.3 on page 24: *Modelling* is the act of creating a model by creating a model description.

Perspective Definition 2.1 on page 6: A *perspective* is part of a person's cognitive universe that may structure her or his cognitive process when relating to situations within some domain

- by selecting those properties of the situation that are being considered (and, by implication, those that are ignored), and
- by providing concepts and other cognitions that are being used in the interpretation of the selected properties.

Programming Definition 5.1 on page 56: *Programming* is the act or process of creating specifications to prescribe systems for a given purpose.

Referent System Definition 3.1 on page 21: A *referent system* is a system that is picked as a reference. It is the original we refer to.

Semantics Definition 4.2 on page 35: The *semantics* of a system description is the set of systems that the description can prescribe. The language of the description gives the semantics.

Snapshot Definition 2.3 on page 10: A *snapshot* of a system is an observation of the system state at a given point in time. Therefore, it is an object configuration of several objects with their relationships to each other and their concrete attribute values.

Specification Definition 2.6 on page 17: A *specification* is a precise and complete description of a system. It unambiguously prescribes the possible executions of the system in the chosen perspective.

System Definition 2.2 on page 10: A *system* is a changing set of active objects that interact with each other and with objects in the environment of the system. Objects may be existing entities like devices, and they may be entities that have to be made. This way, a system is a set of possible executions, i.e. a set of system snapshots that exist at different time points.

Validation Definition 3.6 on page 27: *Validation* of a model is the comparison of some selected model executions with similar executions of the referent system to ensure the model's accuracy.

Verification Definition 3.7 on page 29: *Verification* of a model is the comparison of the whole model with all executions against its referent system. The comparison can be done formally using mathematics if the specifications of the two systems are formal.

Index

Definitions are indicated in bold, and the glossary is referenced in italics.